THE PRINCES

Opposite Order of the Golden
Fleece in diamonds, made for
Maximilian III Joseph of Bavaria,
Munich, 1761.
Frontispiece (overleaf)
The Apotheosis of William
and Mary, painted by Sir
James Thornhill in the hall of the
Royal Hospital at Greenwich
around 1700.

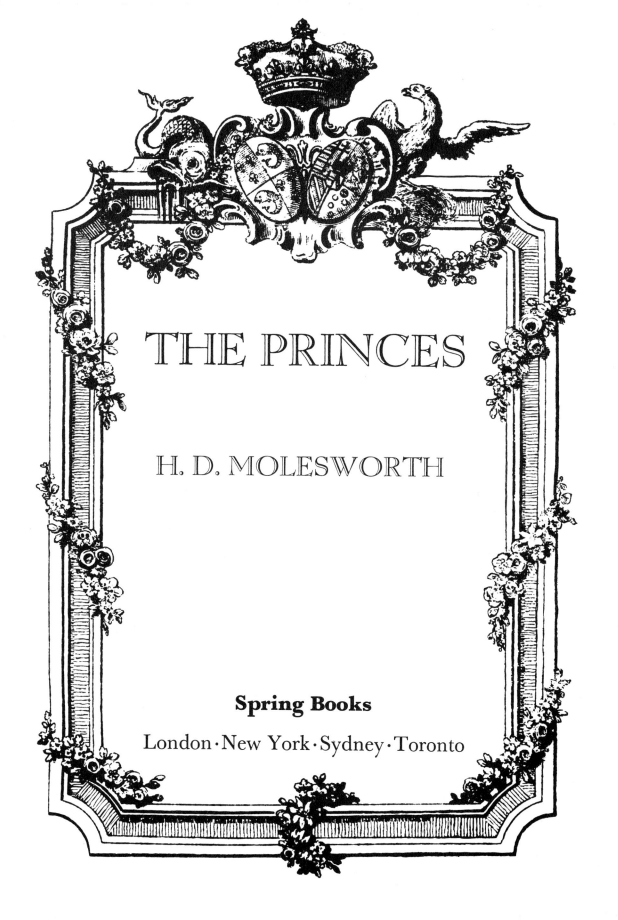

THE PRINCES

H. D. MOLESWORTH

Spring Books

London · New York · Sydney · Toronto

This edition published 1974 by
The Hamlyn Publishing Group Limited
London · New York · Sydney · Toronto
Astronaut House, Feltham, Middlesex,
England

ISBN 0 600 33902 5

Printed in the Canary Islands by
Litografia A. Romero, S.A., Santa Cruz
de Tenerife, Canary Islands (Spain)

Contents

Serenissimus

Over the last century and more the English-speaking world has generally believed that the only tolerable government, as well as the most satisfactory, is that exercized through elected parliaments and congresses, with or without a constitutional monarch. For them it has become almost impossible to accept even the idea that rule by one single person, endowed with absolute power, can be other than morally wrong and politically unsound.

In Europe by the second half of the seventeenth and during almost all the eighteenth century, the vast majority of people never thought in other terms than that all monarchs were divinely sheltered, that their power should be absolute and that this system was correct. Our theme is to show something of how these rulers lived and acted, and something of the arts that they promoted.

The dangers of dictatorship, as we now call it, have been so overwhelmingly displayed that we forget what great advantage can accrue from rulers who can cut through tape, can take decisions and regard this as their birthright and their privilege. Many councils and more businesses are managed on this principle and flourish so long as the leaders have the general interest at heart. This was the baroque way.

There is, or at least till recently there was, a small panelled reception room in the airport at Houston, Texas, decorated with a range of fair-sized colour photographs of leading citizens. The names were neatly printed under each photograph, but in case there should be any doubt about their purpose, a plaque effectively informed the passerby that these folk were 'The Fifteen who made Houston tick about 1955'.

This must be one of the last baroque inscriptions in history. The totally unabashed statement of power, the calm assumption – in the most literal sense – of power, is such as can rarely have been seen in this mid-century. The slogans and photographs of dictators and presidents are vote-catching. Official portraits and stencils of the former may be intended as a warning to critics as well as an icon to the faithful, but their very existence admits – as do the occasional elections – of some moral right to opposition. Even this concession, slight though it may be in practice, did not occur to baroque princes.

Ever since time began, it seems that leaders have worn some distinguishing headdress. As a tribute to the distinction these conveyed, they were normally made of the finest materials and the most valuable jewels. This lovely gothic crown from the Treasury at Munich is thought to have been that of an English queen. Whatever its source it epitomizes all that a crown should convey: dignity, honour, exclusivity and, above all, the serenity of Highness, confident in its own birth and in the especial grace of God.

All the honours and titles which were dependent on birth and history could be recorded in the language of heraldry. To those who could read it – as anyone of importance would – the whole glory of the Hapsburg dynasty was proclaimed on this herald's tabard of the Holy Roman Empire from Vienna. The tapestry from the Pitti Palace in Florence (*opposite*), on which the Medici arms are born by angels, shows a typical combination of artistic purpose, functional use and dynastic symbolism.

The twentieth century may have shouted 'Heil Hitler' or 'Viva Il Duce' or more humanely 'I like Ike', but few even of the most extreme followers would dream of using a word like 'Serenissimus' in any present context. In the seventeenth and eighteenth centuries people did, and such words had real meaning. Intellectual opposition to the system, criticism of Divine Right and even demonstrations by a desperate poor might occur, but there were very few monarchs, however psychologically disturbed, who were not entirely *serene* in their assumption of absolute power and their right to it. Almost all profoundly and sincerely believed that they existed as sovereigns by right of birth and through the direct and considered intervention of the Will of God. Their own and their subjects' belief was conditioned from birth. This was the 'Mystique of Royalty' and treason to it was punished with all the severity that a very cruel justice could devise. In effect, as well as words, the absolute ruler was omnipotent. Unless a religious or social conscience interfered, which was not unknown, nothing but realpolitik would

curb their appetites or instincts, good or bad. Whether their subjects liked it or not, it was these princes and their principles that made the world 'tick', to use the Houston phrase, and it was not until the French Revolution that any more than a handful of intellectuals could think – let alone write – with Tom Paine, 'If I ask a man in America, if he wants a King? He retorts and asks me if I take him for an Idiot'.

The Mystique of Royalty

This bronze statuette of Max Emanuel of Bavaria was executed by Willem de Groff in 1714, years after the victories it commemorates, at a time when the Elector was in exile. The pose epitomizes *Gloire*, that untranslatable essence of all that was greatest in baroque monarchy. This does not mean 'glory' in its usual limited sense, but rather as a Christian would have used the word 'Glory' in reference to God. It implied not only the fame of great estate, or great birth, or even great achievement. It embraced all these and, too, the virtues that went to make them. It was the very essence of prince-liness, yet it might demand that a prince should subordinate his personal desires to the needs of state or even the demands of *gloire* itself. Racine's play *Berenice* is perhaps the best illustration of this curious phenomenon. The spirit behind contemporary royal apotheoses is not unrelated.

In 1694 a small book was published anonymously entitled 'An Account of *Denmark* as it was in the year 1692'. In this was a chapter 'The Manner how the Kingdom of Denmark became *Hereditary* and *Absolute*'.

The essence of the story is this. At the conclusion of peace in 1660, the king thought fit to appoint a meeting of the three estates at Copenhagen 'to try to reduce affairs to some order'. The first need, as ever, was for money, but 'the nobility were for maintaining their ancient prerogatives of paying nothing by way of tax'. The burghers 'thought they might justly pretend to a new merit in a state which they themselves had so valiantly defended'. The debates grew heated and at one point the word 'slaves' was used instead of 'burghers' by one of the nobility. This was enough to spark the revolt. The burghers voted immediately to wait on the King 'and offer him their votes and assistance to be ruler of the realm, and that the succession should be by inheritance, not election as before'. The king 'whether from piety or weakness' thought it dangerous both for them to give, or him to receive such power 'as might be abused in future times'. But he was overruled by the more 'Ambitious and Masculine Spirit' of the queen and opened negotiations. Intrigue began. The king thanked the Commons but said that he could not constitutionally accept their proposal without agreement from the nobles. The burghers set about to remove this obstacle. The mob was raised, the city gates were shut and a march made upon the assembled nobles. These 'saw they were no longer the Masters; the Commons were armed; the Army and Clergy against them' and so they decided after some debate 'to approve what they could not hinder'. 'Thus the great affair was finished and the Kingdom of Denmark in four days time changed into as absolute a monarchy as any is at present in the World.'

Writing thirty years later, the author adds as a postscript that 'The King has taken such care by reducing Ancient and Rich families to a low estate, by raising new ones, by making all the People poor in Spirit, as well as purse, that thirty-two years has had an effect conducing to his purpose [absolutism] as much as three hundred could have done'.

As the writer further emphasizes, this story and its postscript epitomize the movement that had been going on in varying degrees over the whole of Europe during the preceding two or three centuries. By the middle of the seventeenth it had crystallized into a general acceptance of government through absolute royal decree, whatever remnants of parliaments there might still be. The idea, besides being realpolitik, was supported by philosophers with views ranging from reasonably valid argument to the most turgid mystico-religious statements so beloved of writers of the time.

Hobbes in his *Leviathan* supported a monarch who must rule completely, but at least some arguments are brought to justify the principle, if only that even the worst despotism is better than anarchy. Far less lucid and reasonable were the assertions of Sir Robert Filmer, another English 'absolutist philosopher'. His pronouncements found great favour in his day, and even so great a thinker as John Locke felt himself bound to discuss them later in the century. If oversimplified, the gist of his contention was that God had given absolute authority to Adam over his descendants, an advantage which had passed, somehow, via biblical personalities such as Noah and his sons, Ham, Shem and Japeth, to land in the lap of contemporary sovereigns. Quite a lot of arguments went on in such a manner. In Sir Robert's own words 'This lordship which Adam by creation had over the whole world, and by right of descending from him the patriarchs did enjoy, was as large and ample as the absolutist domination of any monarch which hath been since the creation'.

There were, of course, opponents, but the system found more general acclaim than opposition, especially in areas where a feudal tyranny still persisted or where the ravages of war made almost any hope of stability desirable.

In order to find the origins of all this, we must go back in history to the half millennium between the fall of Rome and the eleventh century, a confused period we tend to miss in history books, although as long as from Columbus until the present day.

During this time, out of the warring confusion of Angles and Saxons, Vikings, Celts, Gauls, Franks, Moslem invaders and all the rest, a hotchpotch of their tribal practices was grafted on to what remained of Roman law and custom. We simplify and call the resulting system 'feudal'.

Whatever the maze of detailed practices included in the term, and in the different areas of Europe, this evolution favoured two essential principles: first, that of setting up a sovereign leader chief, with dues of deference; and secondly, acceptance of a privileged group of families with special rights to land or service, but owing an allegiance to the sovereign.

In earliest times the so-called 'kings' were fairly numerous and were usually elected, but as the centuries passed the greater tended to absorb the less and sought to make their states hereditary. The gradual emergence of England as a single 'kingdom' is a case in point. On the continent, the genius of Charlemagne created a pattern of order, and his successors could at least claim to act as Holy Roman Emperor, and thus serve as a focus for some form of hierarchy.

Naturally enough, all this time those special families that did not get the kingdoms fought to further their individual dynasties. By the approach of the first millennium a host of dukes, counts, barons, grafs and marquesses, or whatever they might be called, sought more autonomy and an extension of their power by taking from each other or from the crowns. The sovereigns, reasonably enough, set out to curb this movement, and in turn to swallow up the dukes and barons with their fiefs and dues. Intrigue and warring were incessant. To this foundation the roots of baroque monarchy descend, for in the end the sovereign princes triumphed, to reach the apogee of their power in seventeenth- and eighteenth-century ideas of absolutist rule.

As the feudal development brought some temporal design from dark-age chaos, so Christianity emerged as universal church. In mediaeval times church and state were often at loggerheads. Power lust was by no means limited to lay potentates; popes and great bishops sought for earthly power. Since most people had strong superstitious or religious faith, the church had an initial advantage here. None the less, it needed soldiers as an aid to weapons like the interdict and excommunication, and because of this mutual need and fear of God or the hereafter, a kind of partnership grew up, with love and hate in busy interchange. This lasted until the Reformation split the holy power and Protestant and Catholic set out to fight one another, under guidance of their kings, instead of acting as a single unit against temporal authority.

From the personal and individual point of view, the earlier ambience of thuggery, however modified by mediaeval Christian thought, demanded ruthlessness and energy in rulers. Theories might be interesting and even useful, but it was the exercise of power and personality that kept a man ahead. This, and the fact that mediaeval kings and princes were almost always away at wars, which they would conduct in person, not only made certain demands on them but on their entourage as well. While some followers with brains were necessary, skill and courage in battle, loyalty and the contribution they might make in arms or men were criteria by which the prince had often to choose a number of his men. Apart from the grand parade at courts, the circumstance was often rough and living hard. Kings and knights who had fought and travelled side by side almost ceaselessly could not have many secrets from each other – at least as men; and exceptional expedities like the Crusades might bring an even greater intimacy. In this small world the leading people were thus thrown together, and, apart from ties of feudal loyalty, which often tended to wear thin, only mutual respect – which might mean fear – and mutual need, could keep the system going. While profiting from Christian benediction and their heritage to look upon themselves as in command, the princes were, in fact, obliged to lead as men, relying on men and ruled as men by individual strength and consequence of battle.

But all this was to change as the kings absorbed more power and, as we saw in Denmark, the crown and burgesses allied against the crumbling aristocracy. Centralization gathered momentum and by the 1600s the present lands of western Europe had taken shape under independent and effective sovereign heads, though in central Europe, as in Italy, the Middle Ages game had not been quite played out, and several hundred petty princelings still pretended in the older way. A few of the larger units there could make allies of some weight, but the vast majority were too small to be effective in the outside world, and the real conduct of affairs in Europe came to depend on a handful of the leading kings.

In such circumstances the social system altered radically. The focus of government was no longer a peripatetic command headquarters but the palace in a capital; the minister, the diplomat, the courtier, took the place of noble warrior companions; a new administrative machine grew up to serve the monarch at its head. But perhaps the most important change of all was in the personal approach of princes to themselves. As more and more power fell into their hands, their demands and self-esteem grew so great that by baroque times it could be written and really believed that: 'Kings are absolute monarchs and naturally have full and free use of all property whether lay or ecclesiastical to use for the best need of the state.' The quotation is from Louis xiv, but could be from a dozen others, including England's James i, who readily claimed both property and life, and was not fussy as to whose advantage it all went so long as he got his share first. Early in the field, he had no difficulty in measuring his own desires not *with* those of the state but *as* those of the state. '*L'état c'est moi*' may not have been his phrase but was certainly his philosophy. Such sentiments were destined to become the guiding lines of more and more crowned rulers as the decades of the 1600s passed, and where the greatest led, the lesser postured in their wake.

If the practical steps towards absolutism may reasonably be simplified, the philosophical and legal complexities that came to be associated with the theory of 'Divine Right' in the climate of seventeenth-century thought were strange indeed and beggar any such simplification.

Together with insignia such as the crown, special seating was part and parcel of the trappings of monarchy. To emphasize the sovereigns' apartness their thrones were expected to be larger and certainly of more magnificent material than any normal person's seat. The historic coronation throne of Denmark in the Rosenborg Castle was made in ivory by Bendix Grodtschilling around 1665. The accompanying furniture includes three silver lions attendant on the king—perhaps a typically baroque allusion to the ivory throne of King Solomon, which was guarded by nine silver lions.

Throughout history a religious ritual had generally been associated with the accession of kings. In almost every area a formal mystic ceremony of coronation was made the culminating point. For many, though by no means all, the right to rule was not conveyed until this moment, which represented an acceptance by the new king of God's rule and His Church, and which brought their mystic aid and blessing on his temporal affairs. In the case of elective titles this additional respectability was an obvious advantage, strengthening the princes' claims to be there 'Dei Gratia', by Grace of God, as well as choice of man.

Though one or two elective thrones remained until baroque times, including that of Holy Roman Emperor, the great majority had become hereditary. This gave additional security, and brought with it a new attitude. With the growing claims of absolutism, the Divine support, which had formerly been prayed for as a grace, became 'Divine Right', with a mist of confusion as to how far the Divinity might be inherent in the monarch as well as God, and whether the 'Right' was not now an automatic right of heritage rather than the extension of spiritual grace. Since the whole issue was based upon intangibles drawn out of myth, religion, or long-forgotten history, the field for claims and speculation was unlimited, and the contenders took advantage of it.

In such circumstances it is little wonder that the princes of Europe came to imitate ancient autocrats and sought some sort of apotheosis. This had a classic precedence and crystallized accumulated trends from history which sought to vest royalty with the supranatural. Unfortunately for those with the most extravagant pretensions, Christian monotheism did not admit co-regents with the Trinity, so that something had to be found as an alternative to the godship of the Romans or the pharaohs. The compromise lay in an elaboration of the theories evolved about the sanctity of royal descent.

The idea that 'Blood Royal' – which presumably meant royal genes – was possessed of something special, like a petrol additive, and transmitted an essence different from, and superior to, that of ordinary people, was not new. It was common to many civilizations. But, fact or fiction, the principle had come to be accepted by baroque times as the justification for royal rule. Despite the maze of illogicality and inconsistencies, there were few who did not believe in it – as many do today. The mystery that surrounds the title of 'Highness' or 'Majesty' sets the bearer apart, whether he has just left a mud hut, exile or a palace.

For many people quite a minor Royal is held as a different and, in some way, as a better being than a president of the United States or Russia. This is our heritage of the mystique which ruled the western, as indeed the eastern world, for centuries.

With crowns, as with coronation, there was a curious combination of tradition and modernity, of religious and worldly interests. Originally it was a temporal affair, but the mediaeval Church had almost succeeded in making coronation at the hands of a priest an act of homage by the king to God and, by inference, to His Church. It was not for nothing that Napoleon, though he required the presence of the Pope at his coronation, crowned himself. Manifestly, tradition was inherent in the insignia itself and most monarchs sought to retain at least old jewels, while resetting to their own taste or size. An example is the crown of Louis XV. The stones (now replaced by imitations) were historic pieces and the new setting was made by the most fashionable court jeweller in 1722.

Between them these two photographs present far more dramatically than any words the two basic attitudes from history which coloured the education of most baroque princes. On the one side was the romantic, handsome, crusading knight of chivalry, with perfect courtesy, restraint and manners. Likely to be nicknamed 'the Good' or 'the Fair', such princes entered folklore to become the schoolboy's hero. The Rider from Bamberg *(left)*, carved about 1250, is the very embodiment of this ideal. The second portrait, of Richard II of England from his bronze effigy in Westminster Abbey, belongs to the next century and to a type which is the antithesis of the Rider. Shrewd, impenetrable, all-seeing, machiavellian, it is the quintessence of calculating ruthlessness. More likely to be feared than loved, such people seldom lacked respect. Baroque absolutists' subjects expected their rulers to have something of both qualities, preferably, perhaps, the first at home and the second for affairs abroad.

The importance of a genealogical justification for dynastic claims had developed into a virtual ancestor worship by the 18th century. The 'Gallery of Ancestors' at Munich *(above)* offered imaginary portraits of Wittelsbach forbears in the most elaborate setting, designed around 1730 by Effner and Cuvilliés. The contemporary altar-type tabernacle by Andreas Thelot *(opposite)* bears cameos of the same worthies. Perhaps national as much as family pride is inherent in the 18th-century Czech monument *(opposite bottom)* to the hero King Ottokar II, dead five hundred years before, at Zlatá Koruna.

Once the social principle was accepted, the question naturally arose as to what 'Royalty' might be. While effective wealth and power were obviously desirable, the extent of their possession has never been an absolute criterion for royal pretence. Heads of the greatest nations are – in name at least – equated with the rulers of small sheikdoms of a few square miles. In the Bible, in Roman and other histories these titles are scattered with equal liberality and breadth of significance. We still do the same.

Outside the long tradition of royal apartness, in many areas of Europe the idea of an exclusive caste had been accepted even from tribal times. In most Germanic lands the kings or leaders could only be elected by and from some type of *edelfreien,* a group of special families who gave themselves all sorts of attributes, setting themselves above the commonalty, refusing to intermarry with them, or losing status if they did. From the successful heirs of such as these the German princes rose, and claimed their 'Highness' as a race apart. After Charlemagne they were loosely banded in a Diet, nominally led by an elective Holy Roman Emperor.

There is no clear and open answer as to exactly how all this developed, but as good a one as any is included at the opening of Debrett's Peerage, where the great jurist Camden is quoted on the 'many rights and privileges peculiar to Majesty': 'Some of these are held by positive or written law, others which by right of custom, by a silent consent of all men without law, prescription of time has allowed and the King justly enjoys.'

In such a way it had come to be accepted, even by mediaeval times, that existing kings and certain other princes were of the mystic blood. How they came by it was not too deeply sought, and convenient genealogical fantasies were drawn up by historians. For the greatest effect a line was normally traced so far back in history that fact and fiction were too blurred to matter, though a pause at some outstanding figure such as Charlemagne was held desirable. The Wittelsbach *Ahnengalerie* at Munich is a perfect rendering of all that could be asked. Here the first 'king' within the family was traced to the sixth century, and Charlemagne and another emperor make up the others of the central portrait group.

In many issues logic and political expediency raised a number of very awkward points, and one of the earliest needs of princes was to establish formulae and try to codify their rights. Genealogies, often of very questionable accuracy, sought to decide at what point the mystic quality had come to any line. Then, it was necessary to decide at what stage it died out. Was it inherent and transferable in the female as well as male line? How much, if any, merit could be transferred if only one parent was of royal stock? From the answers to such problems as these were formulated the rules and traditions of absolutist society.

One basic trouble was that any wide approach threatened the limitation and exclusivity which lay at the root of absolute design. The very insistence on genetic transfer threatened it enough. There was likelihood of debasement if too many people came to have a valid claim to royal style and royal pretension, since any descendant of properly mated Royals should presumably, in logic, be in a position to claim this exclusivity for generation after generation. Such an interpretation was inconvenient politically and menaced the great excuse for blood inheritance, which was that it avoided the internal wars of rival claimants.

To keep the system going and maintain the sanctity and purity of royal descent a number of precautions had to be taken. As with the *edelfreien*, tradition and even laws usually prevented princes and princesses from marrying outside the circle or without consent. Morganatic marriages were everywhere discouraged, as tending to contaminate the precious essence and the line's exclusivity. In the ideal, the royal grace was held as most desirably transferred through an unbroken line of eldest sons. Unfortunately the quirks of nature did not allow for such a lack of ambiguity. People died, or were barren, so that modifications had to be introduced if order and dynastic heritage were to be maintained. A lack of living sons meant that some more distant relative had to be sought. Even female succession was almost everywhere accepted by the eighteenth century, and since the monarch was no longer needed personally to go to wars this did not matter. Even a bastard might be considered on a rare occasion, though not accepted. All such concessions naturally raised questions of the basic principle. In practice, the answers to succeeding conundrums were provided by realpolitik and, as with many other awkward questions on credulity or logic, by appeal to God.

Through his vicars upon earth – whatever the persuasion – not only was coronation sanctified, but the irreconcilable could here be reconciled; illegitimates made legitimate; divorce declared a virtue not a vice; or any other little infelicity that might imperil the success of an expedient heir ironed out. Yet here again, both personally and politically, there were dangers in too strong appeal upon this court. It could lead to a revival of the old ecclesiastical demands in temporal affairs. If carried to its logical conclusion, any total acceptance of divine intervention, even at coronation, could prejudice the mystique of inherited omnipotence. After all, the papacy itself, which was monarchy's chief rival in the European power game, preferred an elective succession to one of blood inheritance. This was not unnatural, perhaps, in an institution which favoured a celibate clergy, but nevertheless, since the church could be seen to flourish, the precept might offer a dangerous example.

The ultimate denial of the mystique, by which a commoner might bludgeon his way into the sacred circle, was entirely unthinkable until Napoleon did exactly that, not only for himself but for his family and generals and protegés. The assimilation of these upstarts and the acceptance that they somehow had to be of the sacred blood, and the speed with which it was accomplished, is just another shade of the 'serenity' of Highness and the paradox inherent in the state. However bitter the political differences might be, within a few months of Napoleon's decision to call some Royal and himself Imperial, and with the strength to forward it, Bonapartes and Bernadottes had joined the sacred cousinage of ancient line. More sinisterly revealing was the Wittelsbach approach, which, jackal-like, so fawned upon the new power as to get a kingship for its house. To this degree, the upstart Napoleon was the source of the 'kingdoms' of Bavaria, as well as those of all his other family creatures elsewhere. But if, to make it all respectable, the Holy Roman Emperor could give his daughter to the parvenu – and one divorced at that – could anyone be blamed for profiting by the occasion, especially if rich and grand enough to laugh it off?

Painting and sculpture had often shown mediaeval princes in company with the Madonna or saints and martyrs. This emphasized the contemporary power of Christianity and the acceptance of the church in temporal as well as spiritual affairs. Since the renaissance, a new classical association and background not only reflected wider interests in learning but the change in attitude to monarchy itself. With the general acceptance of absolutism and the sanctity of royal blood – at least on the continent – European princes could as near play gods in real life as they did in the court masques and plays which were a mainstay of their entertainment.

Against this background few things are more significant of the current approach to monarchy than those prints and frescoes of apotheoses, in which the royals, as portly and as plain as in real life, are shown in full court robes, their thrones set strangely on the clouds among members of the classical pantheon. This may strike us as rather odd today, but at the time it was an outward and visible sign of the grace with which the period had come to endow them. Even the pagan element was not without its importance. The reference is not always so obvious as it is in the representation of William and Mary at Greenwich – which must have looked funny to quite a lot of people even at the time. Sometimes the royal features were painted in as Jupiter or Juno or Hercules. In other cases the surrounding company is made up of allegorical figures, representing the arts and sciences, the four corners of the earth or various regions of the kingdom assembled to pay homage. At times the prince might simply be represented by a coat-of-arms or, as at Würzburg, by a portrait being carried up into the clouds.

In any event the attitude is the same. It was well expressed in a seventeenth-century comment, directed to the situation as a whole rather than apotheoses in particular, but none the less pertinent:

As nothing is more pleasant to Princes than to be so deified,
So nothing is more gainful to courtiers than so to please.

The pagan company was also very apposite. It is one of the many paradoxes of the times that although every monarch paid service to God and still claimed – often very devoutly – to hold his honours and his titles 'Dei Gratia', almost to a man – or woman – they rode roughshod over the most sacred virtues of the Christian faith. It is hard, for example, to equate humility with an incessant preoccupation with personal rank or position, while charity had little part in the ever sensitive watch for a trivial slight or deviation from the strictest etiquettes of deference. Yet this lay at the root of the whole system. In this perhaps the church was also to be blamed for the pomp and circumstance with which its leaders were surrounded. The spirit is epitomized by the story of the French ambassador who so far forgot himself in an audience with the Pope as to push the sacred pontiff. Far from turning the other cheek the infuriated prelate just contrived to splutter 'You are excommunicated', and offered not another word. Chastity was an open mockery, at least among the men, and sometimes among the women. Now and then some braver members of a sycophantic priesthood might be led to sermonize, obliquely, but neither they nor anyone else had any very practical effect in making a reluctant prince conform to virtue and monogamy, which was so basic to the creed and which was urged upon the lower orders with penance, whips or prison.

For this race apart any inconsistencies between precept and observance were simply wiped out if whim or pleasure were involved; and most people thought this quite right. But it does suggest that this company was, for the most part, better suited to seek peerage among the jealous, battling, double-crossing egotists that were the ancient gods of Greece and Rome than with any company of Christian saints.

Opposite Always significant for monarchs was the power of the Church, epitomized in these two plates. If the aristocratic archbishop Hohenlohe *(above)* recalls the ascetic personal demands of mediaeval Christianity, the great statue of Pope Julius III spells temporal interests as well.

Faultlessly carved from one sheet of wood, this relief is steeped in history. It was made by Aubert Parent, court carver and soon to be a refugee, in the year 1789. The symbolism is unmistakable: the brave sparrow is a poor successor to the eagles of great kings. An epoch is at an end.

The Royal Person

It was one thing for philosophers to expound theories or to try to justify a particular interpretation of autocracy that events appeared to foster, but it was quite another matter for the few individuals selected for power in this strange lottery of fate to turn these theories into good government. D'Argenson, one time minister and, if perhaps disappointed, an informed and intelligent member of his generation, remarked that 'absolute monarchical government is excellent under a good king', but added 'experience and nature prove that we shall get ten bad ones to one good'. This was a strong indictment of the system, even though the same might well be said of our elected presidents and ministers, with an equal degree of truth.

Whatever might be asserted in the gongaresque flattery of the times, these royal persons were, after all, human beings. They were born and bred of human stock, and a stock that was not always as sound eugenically as might have been desired, whether or not it really had some trace of the royal additives. Their real difference seems to have been their conditioning in 'difference' from ordinary mortals. From birth they were set apart, told they were apart, treated as apart, and, in the end, everyone, including themselves, really thought they were apart. But this conditioning could only be applied to such basic material, physical or psychological, as the parent body could provide and this, over generations, included almost the complete gamut of mental or physical sickness and health, brilliance or madness, and makes the story we shall seek to outline.

At least most could *behave* 'royally' which gave them an enormous advantage in dealing with people. Even today, given some competence, most people would in their heart of hearts, prefer to be ruled by a well poised and well accoutred figure with real breeding, to some balding little man running up and down aeroplane steps in a crumpled raincoat.

In a few, the conditioning and capacities so combined that history sees these royals as something of the figures they were brought up to be. Such princes are not numerous; Louis XIV, Frederick the Great and Catherine the Great remain for us, perhaps, the outstanding autocrats. In their own day they were also

One of the notable features of our period was the general improvement of manners and behaviour. This print by the great 19th-century artist Adolf Menzel for his *History of Frederick the Great* shows Frederick's bully father with his cronies at one of the beer-swilling evenings in his *Tabagie*. One of the last of the old-time, rough, swearing princes of the north, Frederick William carried on his horseplay in the traditional way, but after the example of Louis XIV there were few who behaved like him even when they were not on formal parade. Indeed, as the period advanced, princes seem to have had less and less informality and in the later 18th century there were many who must have acted 'royal' all the time.

admired, at least by such as did not suffer too much from their wars and their taxation, but probably most princes who were not actually maleficent or mental seemed equally splendid in the smaller perspective of their own territories.

But, good or bad, all had one thing in common, they all believed that through inheritance, and some would add 'God's grace', they were the absolute and sole proprietors of their principalities. Some might have a greater feeling of responsibility towards their subjects than others, but this had nothing to do with the principle that they were justified in doing absolutely as they wished. Whether as brutes and tyrants, in the very few cases where circumstances still allowed; or as bewildered heads of states in a position beyond their capacities; as shrewd presidents of their organization; as cosy 'landvaters' – an increasingly popular role in smaller German states; as responsible monarchs, ruling as best they might; as opportunists, exploiting everything for their own selfish pleasure and indulgence; or as power maniacs bent on aggrandizement and battle, all these rulers acted or reacted simply as their natures might dictate. Most liked to claim some moral justification for what they did whether in great issues like peace or war or in minor personal affairs. With some this might arise from honesty or fear of God, with others it was just moral window dressing. One way or another, almost all carried their subjects with them in a sufficient degree so that they could continue as they wished without fear of revolt.

Then, as today, personality and personal glamour could account for much. These were qualities often preferred to intellect or capacity and the settings of monarchy were designed to enhance them. Competence in war still caught the imagination, and by sheer force of personality a leader like Charles XII of Sweden could raise new armies from his tortured country after losing thousands on his mad campaigns. So, later, could Napoleon, or even Hitler. It is a sad comment that the monarchs of enlightenment were so often badly followed when they sought improvement in less glamorous fields, like education, health or the social services. Some might achieve such improvements by strength and imposition but, if they sought for willing and informed cooperation, bigotry and opposition were likely to be their lot, and issues for which they should have been admired were made a target for their critics.

At the outset, Louis XIV's intelligently insolent despotism, coupled with his superbly poised manners, was held by most rulers to be the ideal of personal behaviour and approach. Towards the end of the period, some, like Frederick the Great or the Emperor Joseph II, liked to call themselves 'first servant of the state' or some such euphemism. This was in part a logical development over time, but also a reflection of the advances in political science and philosophy made during the eighteenth century, when much was changing in royal circles. A courtier, possibly the Duc de Richelieu, is alleged to have told Louis XVI that in the time of Louis XIV no one dared speak at court, in Louis XV's days they whispered, and under present Majesty they argued. Apocryphal or not the story sums up what was happening.

Very significant, in the context of the personal reaction even of an 'enlightened' royal approach, is the fact that in his 'History of my own Times', Frederick the Great still refers to historical events, such as wars and treaties, as personal arrangements between monarchs – which, indeed, they still were. The 'King of Prussia' did so and so, the 'Queen of Hungary' or the 'Empress of Russia' did this or that. In distinction, d'Alembert in his letters to Frederick, with whom he was on close terms, refers to the 'French', the 'Germans' or the 'Russians' as doing these things. Deliberate, instinctive or unconscious, these turns of phrase on either side, are indicative of basic attitudes and the changing tenor of the century.

Naturally it is a part of the paradox of princes that for those in their immediate entourage and who met them daily, the person of the prince might intrude upon the mystery of the ruler. What had been awesome at a distance could only too easily become a bore or even funny or silly at close quarters. Particularly in England, with its comparatively recent royal murder, its heritage of Commonwealth and its foreign monarchs after James II, a less sycophantic and adoring attitude prevailed than was general abroad. Though quite a number were prepared to die in the Stuart cause from real loyalty to the prince, whom they regarded as the rightful heir, others took a more philosophical approach. One of these, who witnessed the coronation of George I of England, which ended the fears of another civil war, could write, 'I own I was never so affected with joy in all my life, it brought tears to my eyes'. These were proper, period, king-worshipping sentiments. The well-endowed aristocrat could also add 'and Hope I shall never forget the Blessing of seeing our Holy Religion thus preserved, as well as our properties and liberties'. It was on this same occasion, as the Archbishop proceeded round the throne asking the consent of the people, that an ex-royal mistress and ennobled woman whose interests were biased in other directions, was overheard to declare, very sensibly, 'Does the old fool think that anybody here will say no to his question when there are so many drawn swords?'.

Such robust and human reactions obviously went on outside England too, but the expression of them was likely to be very much more guarded. There was no need to commit a crime to be imprisoned in eighteenth-century Europe, merely to incommode

These two statuettes and the two Medici busts *(overleaf)* tell a great deal about contemporary attitudes to princes. The Netherlandish boxwood figure *(far left)* is thought to show James II when admiral and Duke of York. It is posed with period rhetoric but is reasonably straightforward. The figure of Max Emanuel, perhaps by Willem de Groff, seems to introduce an element of caricature in its exaggeration.

The same attitudes dominate the busts of two of the last of the Medici and serve to emphasize the personal problems of absolutist rule. Religious to the point of bigotry, Maria Maddalena *(overleaf left)* would certainly hold the reins of power, but was unlikely to advance affairs on a broad front. Gian Gastone *(right)* was a pitiful example of decadence and, on occasion, near madness. He could not quite be shut away but he lived in filth, surrounded by roughs and jockeys, whom he had insult him for his fun, and from his palace windows he would buy junk, as a twisted comment on his family's unrivalled patronage. Yet there were few who saw through the system better than this man and he may well have ordered this unflattering portrait as we see it.

the sovereign personally was quite enough. At the least, royal disapproval could mean banishment. This may not sound very much, but Stendhal wrote of it that, 'Louis xiv's chef d'œuvre, which complemented the work of Richelieu, was the invention of boredom *(ennui)*'.

Of the many stories, none perhaps is more revealing of the attitude than that of the courtier returning after many years of exile in the country: 'Sire – when one is unfortunate enough to be banished from your presence, one is not only unhappy, one is absurd.' What seems absurd to us today is that any person, let alone someone of leading rank and wealth, could be reduced to such an abject state, and, what is more, own to it in public. But whether individually true or not, such stories highlight the new interpretation of old principles that brought the princes such advantage.

Tyrannical and autocratic princes were no new thing. In gothic times there was the duke who noticed one of his young courtiers simpering 'in Poitiers fashion' at the duchess, and had the poor boy thoroughly whipped and hung upside down in the castle drain. Such a brutal reaction to a trivial offence, merely because it irked the ruler, should seem terrible to us. Yet the punishment was not unreasonable in its own perspective, and was perhaps more human than Louis xv's dismissal of a minister who lampooned his mistress, or the twenty-years imprisonment without trial imposed on a lesser man for the same imprudence.

As courtiers, the peccants knew quite well what might occur; and yet, foolhardily, they sauced their sovereigns and paid the price according to the times. Early potentates always knew that anyone would get the better of them who could, and so reacted fast and violently to make examples. To later monarchs it seemed impossible that anyone might dare to insult their personal (divinely sheltered) whim, and they reacted from the height of such confidence. Though the eighteenth century could use brutal methods too, they were kept, on the whole, for lower classes.

Naturally, the reality was not so simple, either in theory or practice, but there is a basic truth of argument that it is useful to appreciate.

How, against this background, the monarchs saw each other or themselves, how they felt about their subjects, or vice versa, is a further tale.

Charles vi had been endowed by nature with the qualities of a good citizen but had none of those which go to make a great man. He was generous without discernment, of a limited unpenetrating mind. He had application but was without capacity so that he worked hard and achieved little. He knew German law, several languages, above all Latin which he spoke really well. He was a good father and a good husband

though bigoted and superstitious like all the princes of the House of Austria. He had been trained to obey but not to command. His ministers encouraged him to amuse himself by adjudicating in cases before the Aulic Tribunal [an old German court situated in Vienna] and to absorb himself in minutiae of the ceremonial and etiquettes of the House of Burgundy. Whilst he was fooling about with such trivia or wasting his time hunting, the Ministers – who were the real masters of the country – dealt with everything despotically.

This Prince was inexorable in his punishments. It was the only section of his power that he knew how to maintain with some strength of character.

Mon frère le Caporal!

These quotations are not taken from some twentieth-century communist history but from the highest contemporary comment. The first was Frederick the Great's opinion of the Austrian Emperor; the second the Maréchal, Duc de Richelieu's view of Louis xv; the third, George ii of England on Frederick William of Prussia. Frederick the Great always had something of a guilt complex about Austria, especially after his invasion of Silesia; Richelieu loathed Louis; and George had but little love for his brother-in-law, or vice versa for that matter. Of course, there is always bias, and correspondingly laudatory remarks could certainly be found for each character maligned in these quotations. But, on the whole, they would seem to have some truth and the phrases were perhaps significant about the personalities involved. In essence, there is not much difference between Frederick's contempt and some other lines on Charles: 'He supported himself in every event with an heroic Magnanimity, being always submissive to the Will of That Providence which he knew was the Master of the Fortune of Kings'. As a courtier's euphemism for 'wet' this last takes some beating, and makes Frederick's statement almost kind.

Whatever the justification for these remarks, the significance of the first and last, as of thousands of others that could be provided, is that they emphasize a further paradox, by which all royalty, while adamant and ruthless in defending royalty from any hint of criticism from outside, was itself quite capable of comment, on the man if not the principle. What might have been *lèse Majesté* from lesser sources was but pungent family exchange among the cousinage. Human enough, for most people are ready to criticize their family or country themselves, but are quick to resent anyone else doing so.

Criticism, however, was not what came most readily to the majority of unroyal minds when first confronted with a Majesty. The often quoted passage from Lord Chesterfield still sums up the mass reactions of those who went to court but were not regularly accustomed to its ways.

How many men have I seen here, who after having had the full benefit of English education, first at school and then at the University, when they were presented to the King, did not know whether they stood on their heads or their heels! If the King spoke to them they were annihilated; they trembled, endeavoured to put their hands in their pockets, and missed them, let their hats fall and were ashamed to pick them up; and in short, put themselves in every attitude but the right, that is the easy and natural one.

The answer is, of course, that few people had the self-contented aplomb of Lord Chesterfield. In any event, the carefully calculated formality and etiquettes were expressly designed to bring about this public attitude to princes. It would have been most unsatisfactory if the vast majority of people had not felt as they were meant to feel. This lay at the root of the mystique.

And, indeed, how could anyone have kept up any deep respect in the face of the crashing boredom of court life or the attitudes of those who followed it, let alone the banality of most formal conversation. If royal greetings extended beyond the 'where do you come from' or 'where are you going' of convention they could not, in the circumstance, be expected to go far. If they did, the results might be as when 'He [George III] complained of the want of good modern comedies, and the extreme immorality of most old ones. "Was there ever" cried he "such stuff as a great part of Shakespeare? Only one must not say so ... What, is there not sad stuff? What? What? ... Only it's Shakespeare and nobody dares abuse him".' Torrents of platitude must have poured from royal lips over the centuries. But provided that the speakers could be gracious, every syllable was treasured and the recipients so honoured as to be royal slaves for life. Few are immune, even in this twentieth century.

The quotation about Shakespeare is from Fanny Burney, reporting her first introduction to the court and royal family. Although admitting the conversation was somewhat limited, Miss Burney made no bones about her nervousness and is at equal pains to emphasize how very courteously and discreetly both the king and queen carried her through the early stages. This refinement of manners was not always present in royalty, but it was expected on the right occasions and was always commented on as being most desirable in princes. Certainly all were trained in it and most could turn it on if they so wished and send the stammerer away a grateful witness of their 'condescension'.

Such charm had its obvious political advantages and few, even of the most insolent sovereigns, were completely indifferent to the

The shrewd, sly look given to
George II of England *(above)* by
L. von Lücke in his ivory relief
of 1760, though not as vicious as
the portrait of Gian Gastone de'
Medici (p. 33), is an acute comment
on the man. The emptiness of the
pompous attitude of George I in
the court portrait *(opposite)* by a
follower of Kneller is just because
the painting is bad, and it is a
comment on the period that such
indifferent portraits were found
acceptable and distributed around.

image they presented, especially to persons from outside their
state. None the less there were those whose ideas of charm were
limited; sulks, glowering, or just plain rudeness, were part of the
accepted royal behaviour. A few were frankly drunken, crude
and coarse, especially in the earlier period when roughness still
prevailed in many smaller courts, and princes found it useful to
clout their mates. The later eighteenth century did not approve
and civilized refinement was part of every royal curriculum. Yet
even then a number of the princes found the exercize of self-
control quite difficult and these would rant and rave and throw
things about cursing and swearing. Admittedly such behaviour
was generally restricted to informal hours so that the immediate
family or courtiers might be the only ones to see.

Just as some could be quite impossible, others could be very
courteous and even cosy when not on parade. These would discourse with friends or visitors as gentlemen, though any hint of
familiarity in return would be likely to receive an instant snub or
straight dismissal. At the same time, those so honoured were
expected to behave as friends rather than subjects. With certain
touchy characters this balance was not always easy. Many royals
seem to have had some lesser member of their households, perhaps
a governess or tutor, a valet or gardener, a huntsman or nurse,
who was especially dear and trusted and whose affection for the
royal as a man or woman, was both sincere and deep. In a world
of distrust and intrigue such people must have been most welcome,
and they seem to have been able to do and say anything with their
princes or princesses.

Personal contacts with middle or lower classes unassociated
with the court or the household were virtually non-existent. An
occasional chance encounter on a journey or out hunting might
afford some exchange, but mostly they were just faces at the coach
window or at a civic reception. Many princes scarcely regarded
such people as human; 'the masses which, for the King, do not
exist'. At the same time most monarchs made some political attempt at public showings to keep the people loyal.

For the greater part, the middle classes were unquestioning in
favour of royalty and the basic reactions of loyalty were still
strongly felt. The system was that to which they were accustomed
and in which they had a place of more importance than the mass.
This carried social satisfaction and the form of government maintained the circumstances in which they could traffic and grow
prosperous. Intellectuals might criticize, and need upon occasion
to be put away or ruled against, but they were few, and most
among the bourgeoisie were better satisfied with circuses than
threats. These first they got on state occasions or on such depu-
tations and progresses as took the prince across their path. Then,

for the more important, there could be a chance to bow before His Highness or His Majesty or take some part in a reception. For those even better placed, some small office or a minor title might arise from royal gift. All these things were looked for in the provinces as eagerly as at the court or in the capital. For those not in trade there was the possibility of office in the civil service, or the church, or higher education. In this way a background of middle-class support could be achieved and if rumours of misgovernment, intrigue or squandermania reached them, the impact was not usually very disturbing, for by supporting church and state they helped themselves and their privileged position. Even where they might, by tradition, have elective powers, these were of small significance in absolutist times. Provided they made taxable money and promoted industry, such persons were encouraged, albeit held in slight regard.

Royal contact with the masses was an even more amorphous affair. For harnessed groups like the soldiery some sort of relationship might be maintained, since the mediaeval oaths of personal loyalty were still pronounced and felt. Besides, their loyalty had practical political significance. The rest were but the chorus of the opera. 'Serfs and cannon fodder' to many or 'My People' to the newer father figures, the proletariat were at best children, if not cattle, and properly treated as such. In reverse, the monarchs were a focus of fairy-story remoteness. In times of the greatest distress they might be viewed with open hostility and insults would be hurled, songs shouted in the streets or even carriages bespattered. But, in general, it was the bailiff and the taxman, the press gang and the corvée who were the ever-present and far more real enemies. Indeed, there was often a simple, rather touching idea, that if the worst came to the worst, the prince would appear in his golden coach and make everything right again; a persistence of the mediaeval intimacy. The fact that, on the rare occasions when the people were silly enough to try to put such theory to the test, the answer turned out to be grapeshot, never entirely dispelled the legend.

At other times, like princely weddings or similar junketings, a wave of loyal sympathy might arise. Then horses would be taken from carriages and a host of sweating, cheering populace would take their place; copious sentimental tears would be shed by onlookers and royalty alike, and revolution staved off that much longer. Not that anyone took such considerations very seriously until 1789. Normally it was 'Hurrah for His Majesty', 'Long Live the Prince', 'God Bless His Majesty' and a round at the King's Arms or the King's Head to toast the old loyalties of leaders and the led.

Romantic figures like this Derby biscuit group of a shepherd *(above)* served to remind the privileged just how happy all their subjects were – a blindness as likely to be due to unawareness as indifference. To remind them of their princes every home or cottage had some loyal token, like the engraved glass toasting Queen Anne *(below)* or the lead toy soldier of Frederick the Great *(opposite)* made in 1775 by J. G. Hilpert.

The Setting

All the new developments in the concept of seventeenth- and eighteenth-century royalty obviously called for suitable backgrounds. If mediaeval castles had been vast it was because they needed to house and protect hundreds of retainers; the immediate household and their numerous servants, attendant knights, women, pages, soldiers, their baggage and their horses, dogs and equipment. If these castles happened to impress the populace with their size and strength, it was almost an ancillary virtue, and if they had architectural beauty it was more likely to be due to a successful resolution of functional needs rather than to considered aesthetics. Renaissance princes added conscious – even self-conscious – taste to their establishments, with deliberate propagandist intent and in tribute to their consciousness of their own significance. For the north, unhappily, size and rather crude, lumpy, decoration seems to have been preferred to elegance – a knobbly mountain like Frederiksborg cannot fail to impress by its sheer scale, though Chambord manages a better blend of acreage with care for taste in detail.

By the later seventeenth and eighteenth centuries the interplay of the *zeitgeist* of absolutism and the newer classical styles in architecture were combining to produce a happier visual result in palace buildings. Inside, as outside, elegance, order and dignity were being introduced – at least as far as the façades and the state apartments were concerned.

Versailles is perhaps the most famous of such palaces, and the most influential model in its time, but the essentials of the movement had begun much earlier in Italy, where the princely and papal families had created for themselves homes of unparalleled magnificence and luxury. Above all, the complete refurbishment of St Peter's in the early seventeenth century, on a scale of decoration and extravagance that had never been seen before, was a spur for any king.

By the beginning of the eighteenth century the mania for palace building had spread wide, and princes and architects combined to excel themselves. It is justifiable to include the former with some emphasis, as most monarchs took a direct personal interest in every stage of the creation of their palaces, many of them being

The palace of Stupinigi outside Turin started, like so many palaces including Versailles, as a development from a hunting lodge. Begun by F. Juvarra about 1730, it was not finished till a good deal later in the century. Apart from the angling of the wings, it still depends, like most great 18th-century buildings, upon fenestration for its decoration and upon a vast symmetrical façade, ranging from a central motif, for its effect.

not unskilled in architecture, which was regarded as a permissible accomplishment. In any event, whether in papal Rome, or Versailles, Brühl, Bruchsal, Schleissheim, Petersburg, Potsdam, Schönbrunn, Charlottenburg, Madrid, Naples or any other of the major architectural masterpieces of the period, size and magnificence designed to stress the significance of royalty represented the whole essence behind their construction. The baroque spirit had a new slant in this as in other fields. It was as if Louis XIV's solemn declaration at the opening of his newly founded Academy had been the motto of each royal builder. 'I entrust to you the most precious thing on earth – my *gloire*.'

If few made so unabashed a claim for immortality, quite a number of baroque princes considered their reputation in comparable terms. The idea of divine omnipotence was no longer a prerogative of the Sublime Porte or oriental potentates of fable. It was to this ideal that western monarchs built palaces which bespoke their self-esteem and their dynastic pretension. In all this the theatrical element showed in great strength; indeed most architects designed for the stage as well, and the one no doubt helped the other.

By the turn of the eighteenth century, palace architecture throughout Europe had developed in a fairly general Franco-Italian classic style; from Stockholm to Sicily all were intent on size and theatre. The example of Versailles, both as a conception and as an overall style, set a bias in favour of this approach. Some areas preferred a little touch of more exuberant Italian sensuality while at the Hermitage or Tsarskoe Selo the sense of theatre was perhaps heightened, though not profoundly altered, by the exoticism of the circumstances.

The German princes, notably those of the south, encouraged a brilliant native gaiety to liven up the formal coldness of the French style, and by the second quarter of the eighteenth century had swung away alone – at least in decoration. Here the ingrained German taste for fairyland and folklore could really find an outlet. Only in a few Protestant areas, such as England or Holland, did a rather bourgeois modesty of spirit temper the absolutist splendour. No doubt economics played a part, but natural tendencies and politics did more to keep their projects in restraint.

Externally, the picturesque design for all these great buildings was basically the same. Huge, generally symmetrical façades, the best sides often to the gardens rather than the street, depended for effect on the placing and proportions of the long windows. Some central emphasis was fairly general; an architectural entrance or a central projection with a cresting or a balustrade presented a point of focus, though at first these were, perhaps, less emphatic than under neo-classicism. While all were large, the grandeur was sometimes obtained by enormous length, as at Versailles or Charlottenburg, at others by a massive square, as at Madrid. The great palace of Caserta was even subdivided in its courtyard into four further squares, though this embellishment was no doubt contrived by the fact that it was designed to house the ministries as well. Functional intentions must obviously have dictated other designs, and these differed according to whether the palace was thought of purely as private housing for the family and court or as a centre of government as well. The formal gardens, with their traditional walks, paths and patterned borders of box and flowers, clipped hedges and pleached trees, played an important part in the general design. The English landscape ideals did not come in till later in the eighteenth century. Curiously enough, the street or front approach to many of these palaces always seems to have been left last, often never really finished, and usually untidy. Prints and pictures from everywhere in Europe tell the same story of piles of building rubble and vast open dusty sweeps, even if the railings were elaborate. Admittedly their use as parade grounds as well as a traffic way for thousands of people and horses was bound to make them messy, and allowing for rain and no macadam, the winter picture is complete. Nevertheless, it seems curious that some strip of tidier frontage was not more often kept.

While these elaborate edifices were intended for hundreds and even thousands to live and work in, the whole focus was turned on the state apartments and the stupendous staircase leading to them. This was generally housed in a great entrance hall going up through two or three stories, often to the top of the building; the German word *Treppenhaus* (stair house) is indeed descriptive. These stairways are symbolic of the evolution of the whole epoch, with their fantastic luxury and magnificence and their squandering of space and money to gain effect. On this scale it was a relatively new architectural feature and, when the queen dowager had renovated her palace at Turin, a wit remarked that what had formerly been a palace without a staircase had now become a staircase without a palace. Whatever else was neglected if time or money gave out, these approaches were finished to the most impressive degree. The scale and refinement of the work in examples like Würzburg or Brühl with their weight of superb carvings, stucco and scagliola, leading up to the most triumphant of rococo painted ceilings all referring to the family, cannot have failed to soften the most aggressive visitor and induce a proper state of awe and deference. Halfway up, even the most poised must have stopped to consider the effect of their costumes, and indeed if their hair and jewellery, buttons or brooches were all in order. Such was the deliberate intention of these constructions, as well as their expression of sheer beauty, gracious living and architecture. With

The greatest palaces did not necessarily go up in one burst of activity. Their sheer size demanded time, and this could produce alterations, especially in semi-official constructions, where successive incumbents were not always of the same mind, or money ran out. At the prince bishop's palace in Würzburg several leading architects and more than one member of the highly cultivated Schönborn family had a part to play in the earlier decades of the 18th century.

The great significance accorded
to palace staircases in baroque
times is shown in these plates.
F. Juvarra's drawing *(top left)*
could as well have been a design
for an entrance such as the stairway
of the Royal Palace at Turin
(top right) as for a stage set.
Luca Giordano's full dramatic
decorations for the Palazzo Medici
Riccardi *(below)* in Florence are
expressive of the boldness of early
baroque decoration.

selected footmen or guards in specially designed uniforms holding lighted candelabra at every step, or every few steps, the picture must have been magical, even if it was – as Swift once said of Windsor – 'bloody cold!'

To heighten the atmosphere of awe, the actual throne room, upon which all this building focused would normally be reached from the head of the stairs by a suite of guard rooms, anterooms, reception rooms and waiting rooms, all in enfilade and culminating in the sovereign's presence.

To achieve their purpose these state rooms naturally had to be of the utmost magnificence. Since they had to hold many people, the decorations tended to be on or against the walls and on the ceilings. The latter for the most part were painted, sometimes symbolically but usually with scenes referring to the family's history and importance. The cornices were usually heavy with gilded carving and stucco work. The walls were likely to be frescoed or hung with tapestries or crimson silk; they might perhaps for the greatest rooms and entrances be panelled in marble. For state rooms such weight and importance tended to

In general, the later the period the lighter the design. Full 18th-century rococo fantasy is apparent in the whimsical little bottom of the girl on the stairs of the Vienna Belvedere *(left)*. The utter beauty and fantasy of Balthasar Neumann's great staircase at Brühl *(right)* is as noble an expression of princely apartness as could be conceived.

45

Nothing but the best, regardless of expense, would do for
18th-century rulers. This great wall fountain at Munich
designed by Willem de Groff was made in gilt bronze.

One of the stoves in the 'Rich Rooms'
of the Munich Residence. Even these gave
opportunities for the finest in design.

persist throughout the period, and there was only a slight lifting of the very heavy seventeenth-century styles with their elaborate ornament and their marquetry or ebony, even silver furniture, which, set against brocades and velvets, contributed such an aura of luxury. All this was designed with one thing in mind – to impress and thus enhance the prince's circumstance of sovereignty.

One eye-witness described the fairly modest, and on the outside rather old-fashioned palace of Düsseldorf as having

an abundance and variety of other things [besides pictures] that are distributed up and down ... Figures of brass of the utmost perfection, copied for the most part from the finest antiques placed upon beautiful tables of Florence [marble]; portable cabinets adorned with excellent miniature or inlaid work; in short an infinite number of other things, that are much to be admired, and render this Gallery truly magnificent.

The public rooms still remained elaborate, even if the newest rococo fashion favoured more light and gaiety, as might be seen at its best in the Reiche Zimmer in Munich, or at Potsdam or Brühl. Tall elegant panels of white or colour were enlivened by rich carvings of flowers and tendrils, birds and fantastic beasts, painted or gilded. These, allied with the long light windows, gay flowered silks and a lavish use of mirrors, ormolu, porcelain and glass combined to create the fairy setting. Towards the end of the eighteenth century, the taste for classical simplicity left it to the architect rather than to the decorator to achieve the effects.

It is essential to recall when seeing these rooms today (and many of them have remained or been restored) that we cannot be seeing them at their best. They were designed as a background for a host of people who would only be admitted in full court dress, whose velvets, silks, embroidery and jewellery contributed their glitter to the room.

Behind the imposing façades and state rooms very different conditions might often exist. The immediate royal family had private suites, but they were often quite modest in size. Outside these, leading ministers and lords-in-waiting might have a small apartment of two or three rooms, as did the favourite mistress. For the rest, living was confused and often squalid. Bedsitters with shared amenities were the lot of many, and since almost anyone at court would have some fairly roomy residence elsewhere, it becomes even harder to understand why they put up with it at all. The smell and lack of sanitation must have been acute, by any standard. Little pots and pans found their way by grace of passing servants into larger containers at strategic points, where the contents stayed until others in their turn came to move the larger vessels down long routes of passages and corridors into middens or the cess cart outside. Fresh air or open windows were not encouraged. To make

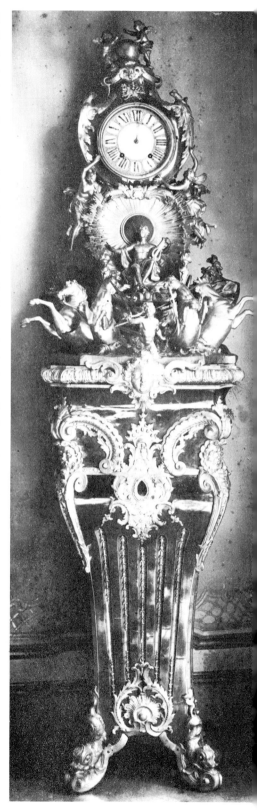

This clock by Cressent, given by Louis XV to the Elector of Bavaria, was an apt vehicle for display.

The great gallery at Schönbrunn. The new lightness and gaiety of rococo could be applied by an artist of genius as readily to a vast gallery as to small intimate rooms.

no finer point, they stank. But as everyone was used to it and made no fuss and nonsense about disinfectants no one was gravely distressed. Disease naturally abounded. Such servants as might sleep in were packed in garrets and cupboards or under tables where they worked, at times even on camp beds in the galleries. Again, such was the tradition that few minded or even thought to mention it. Like the domestic discomforts in wartime, when one becomes acclimatized – which happens very quickly – fastidiousness goes, and the whole thing falls into a new perspective.

It was a combination of comparatively limitless funds, quite unlimited service (albeit some of it a little primitive), and a complete indifference to draughts and cold, that enabled kings and their architects to create with unworldly extravagance. The maintenance and building costs were crippling even for their time, and all these lovely places in no way helped the economy. Even Louis XIV in his testament, urged his heir to restrain this compulsion to build.

Comparative prices are tricky and misleading for different periods but some idea is offered by the calculation that the Duke of Zweibrücken, for example, is said to have laid out fourteen million gulden on a new country *schloss*, this figure amounting to nearly ten times the annual income of his tiny state. Catherine the Great records that accounts existed for over one and a half million roubles for the building of Tsarskoe Selo and that the Empress Elizabeth added more to that. This was only the summer palace; others were being built as well. Something of the significance of this is shown if we remember that a serf might be valued at a few roubles.

Frederick the Great's comment to d'Alembert about his building is significant in several ways and worth repeating. 'May the devil take the glory of war, burnt villages, towns in ruins, thousands of dead, thousands of unhappy people, fear and misery everywhere – my hair stands on end. Potsdam, that is what I need to be happy ... The state does not suffer for it.' Here was the new benevolent despotism speaking. He adds 'I should be ashamed to

At Sans Souci *(left)* Frederick the Great saw no harm in lavishing the prettiest garlands and flowers in gaily painted colours all over the walls of a bedroom – which was occupied by Voltaire. More elaborately extravagant, and thereby perhaps illustrating Italian trends in taste, is Piffetti's furniture and decoration in the Palace at Turin *(above)*.

In gardens as well as theatres fantasy prevailed. Satyrs and shepherds, gods and goddesses, stood at the end of vistas or appeared from nowhere in the glades and shrubberies. This exquisite model of Pallas Athene was created by Ferdinand Dietz for the gardens of Veitshöchheim near Würzburg about 1765.

tell you how much Sans Souci is costing me.' How, except by a rather specious, if honestly meant, division between his private and public purse Frederick could feel that it did not cost the state anything is a different matter. Another comment on the cost of these establishments, which displays a pretty rococo humour, is a portrait at Schloss Sünching showing Adam Friedrich von Seinsheim seated before a vista of his newly furbished castle at Seehof, including the garden with the figures by Dietz. Behind him stands his treasurer holding an empty purse turned upside down.

Less formal, though very often built by the same architects and artists, were the exquisite little houses for play, or the hunting lodges which most princes maintained near their palaces and to which they could repair informally, with or without friends. Here the more intimate scale enabled the stucco workers and painters to create with a precious fantasy and sense of theatre that might not have been in accord with the essential formality of full court surroundings. It was particularly in the German examples that the most gracious interior decorations found their expression, as in the unparalleled decorations of the Amalienburg created by François Cuvilliès for the Elector Max Emanuel. Cuvilliès, a Flemish dwarf, had been adopted by Max Emanuel when he was only thirteen. He showed such genius that the Elector sent him to Paris for training and appointed him court architect on his return. As the illustrations show, there can seldom have been a patron so successfully rewarded for his generosity. In addition to the building, Cuvilliès designed every manner of decorative adjunct, doors, locks, furniture and silver, all with exquisite taste and fantasy. The tradition was carried on by Max Emanuel's son, the prince bishop Clemens August, whose hunting lodge at Brühl was similarly decorated with the finest taste and care. It repeated the theme of the Amalienburg in that there was a series of different styles in the one small house: a plaster rococo room, a formal panelled room, a lacquer room and a room painted with scenes of other properties belonging to the prince, in peacock green against a mustard yellow ground. The staircase was tiled with alternate patterns of Wittelsbach lozenges and scenes from falconry. The name of this folly was Falkenlust.

Less ambitious, but often exquisite, were the little toy houses to be found in princely parks and gardens throughout Europe. Many were in the current oriental fantasy, like the Chinese houses at Drottningholm or Tsarskoe Selo. They were used mainly by the women for picnics and little informal parties. More ambitious was Marie Antoinette's *Bergerie* where the court ladies could go and play at shepherdesses and dairy maids and feel themselves like the porcelain figures they collected. In fact the Trianon was more of a separate country palace. In addition to these play houses any prince of quality had several hunting castles in the country to which he would go for sport or relaxation and where the etiquettes were, normally, less rigidly maintained.

In palace settings only the greatest magnificence of dress and personal adornment sufficed. These almost every baroque prince adored, the men as much, if not more than the women. They plastered themselves with sashes and jewelled orders and decorations, gold and silver lace, vivid silks and velvets, embroidery of every richness and luxury of material. Hundreds of pounds might be spent on a single coat or waistcoat, which makes any extravagances of today seem trivial. Saint-Simon claimed to have laid out an equivalent of something like £1,500 on his own and his wife's clothes for a single party, and naturally kings and princes needed more. In addition to personal clothes came all the different uniforms for parades, hunting habits, and robes of state which cost a fortune in fur and velvet in themselves. Every order of nobility of which the king was head in his own state had separate regalia and robes. Even the adjuncts were rare and expensive from the silk stockings down to cambric handkerchiefs. Confuse the issue yet once more by stating that in many courts it was the perquisite of some valet or official, on some occasions, to remove the private wardrobe for his own advantage and it becomes a matter of little wonder that many royal accounts show claims for formidable sums of money in arrears. Economy in this direction was not applauded and a king like George II of England, who hated display, was criticized in print and caricature for unsuitable modesty of dress.

With the robes went regalia, and in the field of jewellery we find some of the most exquisite creations of the day, since it was appreciated not only for the size and water of the stones but also for the settings that could be designed for them. Private jewellery and even regalia were frequently reset and many of the greater stones have fascinating histories which can be followed as they passed from one royal crown to another, or to orders and ornaments and back again. One thing was certain – every prince had as much as he could possibly afford, for it was the public statement of his wealth and his magnificence. But there were few who could rival the kings and queens of Saxony; a small fraction of their collection consisted of complete parures for each in different stones – diamonds, rubies, emeralds, and so on. As each parure for the king included sword hilt, snuff box, buckles, buttons, orders and the rest, and those of the queen, great stomachers, hair ornaments, more buckles, buttons, rings and necklaces, the imagination boggles at the combined value carried by the pair on state occasions.

A vista in the gardens of Schönbrunn.

The Court

The 'court' should be seen not merely as the palace which housed it, nor the sovereign and courtiers who composed it. It was all these and also a way of life, with its focus on the Highness or the Majesty from whom all honours, government, places and profits, leisure and entertainments, as well as life and death, depended. It was also the means by which the absolutist rule could be maintained. Here anyone gathered who was 'anyone' or wanted to be 'someone', in the worldly sense. Some were commanded by the crown, others came by right of noble birth. Middle and lower classes were normally excluded. The hangers-on ranged from ambitious youths to the most questionable opportunists trimming as best they could for any pickings that they might obtain.

To most people today the courtier is likely to be a figure of fun, the tall skinny man with spindly legs and extraordinary ways who bows and scrapes his way across the pantomime stage. Alternatively he may be a short stout man with a preoccupied air bustling about like the White Rabbit in *Alice in Wonderland*. Both caricatures belong to the land of folk-lore and fairy-story and have their origins far back in popular literature. The caricature was perhaps a popular revenge on those hordes of parasites which the people had to support and for whom they were so cruelly taxed. But more serious plays are also full of them.

These two examples draw attention to the types of courtier that did exist. If the pantomime figure is the nobleman attending court for place and pension, the White Rabbit stands in for what might well be termed the 'courtier minister', who had the real work of advising the crown or seeing that his monarch's edicts were obeyed. Though the day-to-day attitudes and conformities may have been the same, their social purposes and often their origins were so different that it is as well to keep them separate.

The evolution of the royal courts was again a logical process. Tribal chiefs had had immediate retainers for friendship or protection, and as mediaeval courts expanded and took more formal shape, the motley of hangers-on needed to have order and control. Titles and status were codified, lists were drawn up and salaries and precedence for the hierarchies established. The Black Book of the Exchequer for England's Henry II is an example.

This plate shows one of a group of paintings (see also pp. 149, 200), now on the walls of Schönbrunn, which were commissioned to record the various stages of the festivities surrounding the marriage of Joseph II. Not only do they show every detail of the costume and of the decorations of the Imperial palace, but, between them, almost every facet of court performance. Here we see the royal banquet. Only the royals and the band are seated. All the rest of this vast throng are standing, and no doubt stood for two or three hours and more before going home to eat something themselves. Yet there were few outside the aristocratic circle who would not have given a substantial part of their fortunes to be so favoured as to be allowed to stand around and watch on such an occasion.

Two courtier types. The great aristocratic Earl of Dorset *(above)*, painted by Isaac Oliver in 1616, shows the ultimate in extravagance. Bernini's bust of Mr Baker has all the self-importance of a thruster on the make.

As well as establishing order on a firm basis, the household books also served as a measure of justification for the royal demands upon the taxes. The offices seem strange to us, but the titles all referred at one time to actual functions. As the centuries passed, many – if not most – of the functions became redundant or were absorbed into the developing forms of civil service, but, although there was everywhere talk of economy at one time or another, very few princes willingly abandoned any post. The places were kept, and many others created, to provide appointments and sinecures by which the monarchs could purchase the interest, if not always the loyalty, of persons to whom they were grateful, or whom – for one reason or another – they wished to keep around them. Something of the picture is gained if we consider that the comparatively small court of James I of England numbered over fifteen hundred members of the household, with the servants. Insofar as they could be counted, the complete Versailles establishment ranged round the five or six thousand mark. Even then such figures are misleading in that they take no account of hordes of casuals, from visiting royals with their suites, to the theatre, ballet or opera companies which might be called upon from time to time.

In addition to the court places and sinecures all naval or military appointments were ultimately in the gift of the sovereign, as were those of the church, at least in Protestant areas. And as more and more provincial administration fell to officers appointed by the crown, this ensured a further chain of patronage. With such largesse to scatter there is little wonder that the leaders of the land gathered at the prince's feet. Even in a constitutional monarchy the system worked, and a ruthless prime minister like Sir Robert Walpole quite shamelessly kept his Whigs in power, partly for the king and wholly for himself, by use of these positions, which the king allowed him to exploit. 'There was hardly a place of profit under the Crown or in the Church, the Army or the Navy that could be disposed of without prior consultation with him.'

The minor offices did not, of course, gain admission to the court itself nor to the immediate person of the crown. Such advantages were reserved for the highest places, normally filled from the aristocracy or the leading families. The right of appointment to the lesser posts, together with the fees accruing from them, often served as perquisites for ministers and favourites. These did attend the court and drew this privilege from doing so. The practice helped to keep the whole machine in motion and reasonably solvent, if not in good financial order.

In such a development, the kings had been vastly helped by economic changes as the feudal system broke down throughout Europe. The section to be hardest hit was the aristocracy; the poor were so poor anyway that it made but little difference, yet every-

The most successful courtiers, like the French finance minister Nicholas Fouquet, made vast fortunes and could build palaces on the scale of Vaux le Vicomte *(opposite)*, completed for Fouquet in 1661.

where the nobles' rights and dues had been whittled away in favour of the crown. Rents brought in less and less and as they took to living at the court, the costs and the extravagances there made further inroads into shrunken estates. As a result families of the greatest pretension were often up to their eyes in debt. On the continent their general refusal to follow the new avenues of prosperity in trade – other than an occasional marriage with the richest merchant families – left little alternative between rotting in the provinces or attendance on the monarch in quest of any place or bounties that he might bestow. The system was perfectly well understood on all sides. Those who served the king well or for one reason or another had the king's favour, were loaded with riches and honours and held the highest places in the new fairyland. Worship at the shrine of the new divinity could be very profitable indeed and was cynically exploited. A good companion at the tables or the chase, or a better one in bed, was regarded quite as highly as the most industrious minister. The utterly cynical exploitation of this power by princes was a salient feature of the day. Some monarchs developed a fine art in bringing a poor creature to the ultimate of debt and ruin by forcing him to keep up with the expenses of the court and then – at the eleventh hour – would come to the rescue with a place or pension, and so buy his loyalty, gratitude and services for life. As the place or pension could be removed at any time by royal whim it was, of course, sheer blackmail. As our first commentator on Denmark noted, the success of the system depended upon 'reducing Ancient & Rich families to a low estate' and 'raising new ones'. Small wonder that when caught in this dilemma the courtier bowed ever lower for his place and fawned and flattered to the basest degree.

Just how profitable direct access to the king might be to any individual is dramatically illustrated in the case of George Villiers, later Duke of Buckingham. Acknowledged by all to have been extremely beautiful and also agreeable, he was noticed by James I of England, in 1614, when he was twenty-two. By 1615 he was knighted, given a pension of £1,000 a year, and made a gentleman of the bedchamber. In three years he had gathered a host of further titles and appointments, including those of Knight of the Garter, Marquis and Lord High Admiral. Naturally enough his own supporters profited too. In reply to critics of his questionable support for this young man James remarked 'I am a man, like any other ... Therefore I act like a man and confess to loving those dear to me more than other men'. He was not 'like any other', he was an absolute king, and one of the first to know it and to practice as he preached.

Spectacular personal advancements apart – and there were many – one of the most interesting phenomena of the whole abso-

For the west 'the Orient' was the fabled end of splendour, wealth, jewels, magic, slaves and, above all, *absolute power*. The Orient might begin at Constantinople and wander indefinitely to Cathay, India and realms of sheer invention. Facts were generally hazy and when the great goldsmith and jeweller Dinglinger was charged to create in the early 1700s a whole court in gold and jewels for Augustus the Strong of Saxony, the commission was no more nor less pure fantasy than fairy tales like Cinderella. Here we see a little group from this enchanting and very expensive toy, said to represent the Delhi court at a birthday of the Grand Mogul Aurungzeb.

lutist revolution of the seventeenth and eighteenth centuries was the speed with which it changed upper-class thinking from that of a potentially militant opposition into a sycophantic formal aristocracy entirely dependent upon the king's whim. It was through the development of the court that this was brought about. The outstanding example was, perhaps, Versailles, but the system was widespread, and even of the English Burke could say in the House of Commons, when attacking sinecures and 'places' in the 1770s, that the aristocracy could as readily 'act the part of flatterers, tale bearers, parasites, pimps and buffoons as any of the lowest and vilest of mankind'.

The fundamental basis of the new social order lay in its exploitation of that simple human characteristic usually known as snobbery. Modern psychology may have different names and explanations, but for the seventeenth and eighteenth centuries it was an organization of the pecking order, by which everyone – except the king – had someone over them to envy or revere, and everyone – except the lowest serf – somebody to whom they felt superior. The maintenance or improvement of that position was the basic aim of life.

As we have seen, feudal society had also had its agreed hierarchies, but there was in fact a great difference of attitude between the sovereign, as head, receiving the sworn fealty (by implication, freely given) of his immediate dependants in return for practical services and territorial function, and the sovereign as head of an entirely artificial structure, alterable only by himself and based chiefly on the accident of birth, without regard to merit, competence or function. If the great lords still paid homage at the coronation, it was merely through a picturesque tradition, the oath was but a formal expression of acceptance of the situation which existed, it was no longer that of an independent person offering his service, sword and honour. In the new order, theoretically at least, any member of the recorded class could, with sufficient trouble, tell at any moment his or her exact position in the hierarchy, with its rights and dues of honour and precedence. In the case of the court group all knew their position exactly, and did little else but bother about it at every possible occasion or seek to advance it by ingratiating themselves with the prince. In fact they paraded their pretensions and quarterings and fought about them so much that duelling had to be stopped by law.

By a fine manipulation of the grades among the upper classes the prince could subdivide and rule, and since the crown alone could alter the situation, the cards were all on its side. On the whole, the monarchs used this advantage with discretion and with sufficient intelligence not to overplay their hand. If the odd bastard or mistress was created a duke or duchess, it mattered

The successful courtier, who in this case wears the robes of the highest English Order – that of the Garter – must have looked exactly as in this drawing by Sir Peter Lely. The curious combination of adoring respect and allegiance in his gestures was presumably directed rather to the King than to God, but in no way interfered with his good opinion of himself. Shown by all these trappings to be one of the great ones of the earth, he was indeed content with his position and, unless very highly born, had probably stopped at almost nothing to reach it.

made upon the whole Court, and in which the Count and Countess were very ill treated; but *Little Kamcke*, who never despair'd of his Success, still continu'd to make his court to the King, without seeming to take the least Notice of the Minister's Ill-will. His assiduous Attendance was at length rewarded; the King begun by granting him the Honor of playing with him every Night at Chess; which was a Favor this young Courtier so artfully improv'd, that in a little time after, his Majesty made him a Minister of State. The Count *de Wartemberg* was mortify'd in two Respects by the Advancement of *Little Kamcke*; for he did not expect such a Favor to be convey'd by any Canal but himself; and besides it was granted to a crafty Enemy, whose rising Credit might well give him Umbrage. *Kamcke* for his own part believing that he was only oblig'd to his own Merit for his Preferment, had even less regard for the Prime Minister than before. They star'd upon one another at first, without venturing to make an Attack; but by degrees they came to high Words; and at length *Kamcke* being puff'd up with his Favor; and being moreover supported by all good Men, he vow'd the Destruction of the Prime Minister, and his Creature, the Grand Marshal. He was so cunning as to engage his Cousin *Kamcke* in the Scheme, because the latter being Great Master of the Wardrobe, cou'd give the Prime Minister the fatal Blow with more Ease than any other Person; and he succeeded happily; for he aggravated to his Majesty the Complaints of the People, and the Murmurings of the whole Court. The Queen too being prejudic'd by *Kamcke*, spoke sharply to the King, who at last consented to the removal

moval of a Minister, whom till then he had thought he could not be without.

This great Scene was open'd by the Disgrace of the Count *de Witgenstein*, the Grand Marshal of the Court, and the Prime Minister's Creature, who was arrested in his House on the 27th of *December* at 10 o'clock at Night, by a Lieutenant of the Guards and ten Grenadiers. Next day, about 9 in the Forenoon, M. *de Gersdorf*, Colonel of the Regiment of Guards, accompanied by *Stossius*, Treasurer of the Order of the Black Eagle, came from the King to demand his Ribban. He presently restor'd it, assuring them that he was wrongfully maltreated; but that nevertheless he did not complain of the King, and that they were only his Enemies who had impos'd upon his Majesty's Goodness to ruin him. Not long after an Officer of the Guards came in and told him, that he had Orders to carry him to *Spandau*. He made answer, that he was ready to go wherever the King commanded him; only he desir'd Leave to write to his Mother-in-law, who was the Queen's Lady of Honor. The Officer told him, that he was forbid to let him speak or write to any Person whatsoever; and then he took him with him into a Coach that was attended by 12 Life-Guard Men.

The Noise of his Confinement being presently spread throughout the Town, a Multitude of People gather'd in a trice before his House, every one crying out against the Grand Marshal, calling him the People's Blood-sucker, and the Author of all their Taxes. When they saw him put into a Coach to be carried to *Spandau* *, their Shouts were doubled; but the Grand Marshal, without being

* See Vol. I. p. 3.

We hear so much about 'intrigue' at courts, but it is hard for anyone today really to appreciate what was involved when one man or woman was all-powerful. Nothing could be balder or more revealing than this contemporary account from an English edition of *The Memoirs of Charles Lewis Baron de Pöllnitz*, published in 1739. No contemporary reader of this gossipy travelogue would have been in the least degree suprised at the narrative presented, or particularly shocked at the apparent triumph of evil; convinced, perhaps, that anyone wronged here had no doubt done the same himself some years before.

little. A few kings openly sold titles, though such nobility was, of course, despised by those of earlier creation.

In such a society, Orders were for many the be all and the end all of desire. There, outwardly and visibly for the world to see, the wearer was distinguished from the herd. As the ultimate, the leading decorations, like the Garter, or the Fleece, or Saint-Esprit, were eagerly competed for by kings and princes too. By and large the ranks were kept sufficiently exclusive to make them still desirable, and, by astute distribution, titles and honours could be made to serve the sovereign cheaply to reward his friends or buy his enemies. All but the grandest could be raised in rank and given one of the more exclusive Orders, which were worth far more to them than money, and cost the crown a pittance. Some minor German princes created their toy Orders too. Within their states these served as usefully as greater ones elsewhere. Naturally they made little stir outside unless with rather caricature snobs like Boswell, who went to the most pathetic lengths to try and get an

Order of Fidelity from the young Prince of Baden-Durlach. He failed, but at least had the honesty to laugh about it, albeit wryly. Most people of the time (as well as many – if not most – today) were quite susceptible to such distinctions.

'We show our quality by our birth and titles, Madam' was one English lady's riposte to a German critic of English deportment. However modest this particular encounter, the statement expressed the principle of the whole system. (For the sake of the story it might be added that her ladyship concluded the remark '... and not by sticking out our busts'.) Nevertheless, it was on the whole by the subtler methods of exploitation that this system was kept going day by day. The formal waiting and attendances were enlivened by the ultimate refinements played by Majesty in person: recognition or neglect of a bowing courtier, particular singling out for favour – a smile, a few words, a nod, a frown ... the innuendoes were endless. Insignificant in themselves they made and kept this tiny world upon its toes. Special invitations to special parties, an intimate evening, or a weekend hunting, were enough to keep the highest in contented servitude. These minutiae were the talk of the court and everyone watched and speculated. In such matters princes were superbly trained and in such expressions almost none would make mistakes. As a final act in the kings against the barons situation the solution was ideal, since it kept a lot of tiresome people quarrelling among themselves about absurdities, instead of plotting against the crown. The techniques have now passed on to chancelleries and boardrooms or the presidencies of control, yet if the adaptations are less refined and the accent often Brick or Bronx, the results are still effective.

In addition to being the fountain-head of all honour and advancement the courts were also the focus and centre of a whole new development of elegant and fashionable life. They provided a world of elaborate entertainment and luxury exclusive to the favoured few, where theatre and opera, masques and balls, gambling and beautiful clothes extended the bucolic outlets of hunting and drink. Luxury and entertainment of this nature had always been associated with royal circles, since only princes could contemplate the huge expense of keeping troupes and orchestras, theatres, writers, and of providing the massive hospitality that went with it all. Renaissance princes had done much in presentation and expense, but, in the course of the eighteenth century, elaboration passed all bounds. As the attractions of this new fairyland were added to the delights of social advancement there is little wonder that all who could made efforts to associate themselves with this especial company.

The basic principle of setting up a central court, to which the powerful could be drawn and so come under princely influence,

An Order of the Golden Fleece 'in diamonds' from the Munich Treasury. Several inches long, this bauble contains some diamonds as large as an adult's thumbnail. Such pieces were a way of making payments for services rendered by one prince to another.

The exquisite and sumptuous elegance of Cochin's drawing of the *Return from the Ball (above)* is a far cry from Frederick William's *Tabagie* (p. 26) and far more in keeping with the new developments of the 18th century. So too is the equally enchanting *Reading from Molière* by J. F. de Troy *(opposite top)*, which once belonged to Frederick the Great. In both the ultimate refinement of self-presentation is the key. Certainly in the case of de Troy's readers not one of them is as interested in Molière as in the figure he or she presents. The little dancing pair by Ferdinand Dietz *(opposite bottom)* serves to recall that in the smaller German courts, however much Versailles customs might be aped, the results could on occasion seem provincial.

was applied throughout Europe, and even held, in a provincial Ruritanian way, for the petty German and Italian principalities. If the quality of life and entertainment was not on the scale of a great national court, the locals did their best, and at least gave a local consequence and entertainment to those about them. In any case, for anyone with the slightest pretension to be civilized the alternatives were very bleak indeed. Just as the gap between rich and poor was enormous, so the difference between attachment to the local prince, even if he was quite modest, was vastly far removed from the rigours and brutality of country life, particularly in winter.

Apart from the opera or the theatre, and the delights of being seen in the right place at the right time, any hopes of intellectual life at the court might well be restricted. Although the standard of upper-class education improved throughout the period, and literacy was becoming general by the end of the eighteenth century, any further extension of mental capacity beyond that of listening to a play, or conversation, was fairly limited. Those who could do more were welcomed by the private salons and the literary clubs, but few courts sought them out. For many with the most quarterings, intellectual conversation was likely to be rather 'bad form', and platitudes, gossip, sport, smut or genealogy were generally preferred.

If the seventeenth century could still be rough, the eighteenth saw many improvements, and it was in behaviour that the changes showed. Among the new desiderata certainly came elegance of mien and manners, beauty if possible, clothes and wit.

He is the very monument of Grace, his every movement of the most fastidious consideration, his lightest word is fraught with meaning and his slightest gesture of significance. He toys with bagatelles, elaborates the slightest thought with infinite dexterity and knows the chart of Gallantry better than all the Scudéry's that ever were.

This description by Frederick the Great in a letter refers to the young Prince Salm who had just returned from Paris in 1781. The comment is not without malice as the king mentions Salm again in a later letter to say that he, Frederick, is getting too old and has to leave the lighter affairs of court life to such as the young Prince Salm with his 'red heels'. At the same time one feels that the jibe is prompted by envy for youth and elegance quite as much as by dislike, and in an introductory sentence he writes that the young prince 'puts me to shame. I find myself so inept, so clumsy, so stupid by comparison, that I can scarcely summon up the courage to reply to him' – a comment indicating that with this sophisticated monarch the envy is even tinged with admiration.

What does seem to have been appreciated by all but the most priggish was wit, for preference a pretty, malicious wit as in the plays of the period (as later in those of Wilde or Coward). The diaries and letters all record the sayings of one or another. By the eighteenth century a sharpness of tongue (if it did not earn a beating, as in the case of Voltaire and the Chevalier de Rohan), might even compensate for some defect of breeding. Real genius for wit was probably no more frequent then than today, though in the eighteenth century the slightest sign of it was cultivated to the limit, whether by peer or playwright.

This is how a Bow porcelain modeller of about 1750 saw a leading actor as the courtier fop in a current play. Many of the bourgeoisie or poorer provincial gentlemen, who could not aspire to reach court life, laughed against such people as much in envy as in genuine contempt.

The witty approach might well be introduced even on the most serious occasion. No illustration could be more vivid than the behaviour of the Duke of Abrantes on the death of Charles II of Spain. The whole world was breathlessly awaiting the outcome of this great heritage of such vital importance to the balance of power in Europe. Coming out of the conference after the king's will had been read, M. d'Abrantes faced the assembled court and ambassadors, as Saint Simon tells us:

He paused with serious mien and looked carefully around, and seeing, finally, the Graf Harrach, envoy of the Emperor, he pressed forward to embrace him [the eighteenth century both embraced and wept a lot without loss of dignity]. He paused, and everyone thought this an omen on the Austrian side. 'Monsieur', (embrace) 'it is with the greatest joy ...' (pause for further embrace) 'and satisfaction' (embrace) 'that I take leave of you for the rest of my life and bid farewell to the House of Austria'.

Not all persons of quality submitted to court regimentation, but the most effective section did. They came either from choice, or because they were commanded, in order to keep them out of any mischief they might do if left at home, for, although this threat to royalty was now dying out, incidents like the Fronde or the Jacobite activities kept kings alert. A few, very studious or earthbound, might while away their time administering estates and dabbling in such books or science as they could affect, but there were few in the provinces as company for discourse or for anything more than hunting and the bottle. Occasionally there may have been amiable old country persons like Sir Roger de Coverley, content enough to squire their acres, but the rest were pretty brutish louts, living little better than the farmers and peasantry about them, whom, of course, they affected to despise. Some nobles were so poor that they could not possibly aspire to attend at court, especially in those areas which had no primogeniture and held to equal subdivision of the property. After generations such families might be reduced to almost nothing but their coats-of-arms. They continued their exclusive privilege of leading men in war, since personal courage was one heritage they had, and this was the only outlet that tradition allowed them, except to enter the church. Yet, even here, since all the best appointments came from Majesty, attendance was enjoined if not upon the prince in person, at least upon a man or woman who could press a cause among the topmost ranks at court. The answer for any who could get there was – the court.

It is not easy for anyone conditioned by the mid-twentieth century to understand the moral any more than all the social or practical aspects of this movement. For the most part these people of the court and the nobility were, quite simply, obsessed by their social rank and honour. To the majority of them it deeply mattered whether they sat above or below a person at a meal or what someone's antecedents were, whether Majesty smiled or a prince of the blood was affable. This was the end aim of their lives. Even the most pious churchgoer would fly into a passion if she or he was misplaced at a formal ceremony. Individually, the vast number of these baroque privileged were doubtless basically as kind or not, as charming, informed, pleasant or unpleasant as in any society anywhere, though the circumstances were strong against the virtues, however they were preached. But at least all were trained to behave. The very civilized and graceful must have been true paragons of elegance, even if they did smell like polecats much of the time, a defect which they sought to remedy not by washing, but by the most extravagant resort to scents.

What may seem a little strange about them, as about the monarchy itself, was that they managed to maintain a way of life which was in almost direct opposition to the tenets of the religion many of them sincerely held. Admittedly religious emphasis was adapted to the needs of so influential a group, from whose ranks the princes of the church itself were likely to be drawn. Indirectly, God was blamed, since it was held that society was so constituted by His will that any discrepancies, such as the ghastly poverty among such wealth, could only be a matter of Divine intent. Nevertheless, while attending church daily and, in conversation, extolling the merits of charity, humility and the rest, most courtiers spent their waking lives thanking God that they were not as other men and trying by every means to get a little less 'like' by aspiring into ever more exclusive circles.

Anyone who attended European courts before the first world war might have seen the old ways still at work, though not perhaps playing so integral a part in constitutional societies. The influence of snobbery in class was very powerful still, and although reduced today, Debrett's Peerage and the Almanach de Gotha do still exist. Their protocols and orders still persist, but as the greater part of the effective people of our world do not belong between such boards, their contribution merely serves to implement a theatre world of some few remnants of the past. It is perhaps in business communities that traces of the baroque attitude remain. There, some 'presidents' or leaders of the civic clubs really strive to give themselves, or feel they have, importance in their own community. Their posturings can be as effective or absurd as any of the eighteenth century when characters like the 'Bourgeois Gentilhomme' and Mrs Malaprop strutted out to bring amusement to the gently born.

Etiquettes

All this splendour and elegance in wonderful settings essentially called for decorum and manners. Jolly horseplay and schoolboy bawdy might accord with the earlier architecture but not with the new classical style or the exquisite refinement of rococo. Nor did it accord with the new approach to monarchy, which these things were designed to enhance. Although in private apartments and when not on parade, royals might, like anyone else, do exactly as they wished, here we are concerned with formal presentation.

Princes had been surrounded by etiquettes ever since civilization began, and there was, perhaps, little that was intrinsically new in the developments of the seventeenth and eighteenth centuries. It was rather the greater spread and greater insistence and greater refinement of conduct that brought the novel elements. The details were so complicated that books instructing chamberlains and marshals in the rules and precedents could run into hundreds of pages.

The roots and origins of some of these are far from simple. Some were inherited from history, through Rome or through Byzantium, through Christian ritual or tribal practice. These included all the traditional acts of deference designed to stress the position of the prince standing at the apex of society. In some, security precautions may have played a part, thus bowing, kneeling, thrones and regalia are reasonable. But many others of the host of baroque state formalities would seem to have evolved from the efforts of succeeding generations at the court seeking to advance their individual status or that of their official post, until every trivial move could have significance and involve someone.

Originally, all posts giving direct access to the sovereign had some real function: the Master of the Horse did organize the stables, the Falconer the falcons, and so on, but as time passed most of these contributions had ceased to be demanded, or, if some administrative purpose still obtained, it was likely to be carried out by an outside staff. The noble holder was only interested in his access to the royal person and his function in the ballet of behaviour in that presence. As such an approach was very much in keeping with the politics of absolutism, the kings did all they could to encourage it among their aristocracy, preferring them to

If the plate on page 52 shows the full ceremonial of a court banquet, this charming painting by Luis Paret of Charles III of Spain at a personal repast tells of the state and formality surrounding simple royal meals. If the attendant courtiers lounge about in fairly easy attitudes, they are there and they are standing and will remain standing until His Majesty has finished. Most will probably be there the next day as well, even the next year. The only ones who seem at any liberty are the favoured royal dogs.

think of trivia instead of insurrection. By the eighteenth century etiquettes had developed such elaborations that many kings and courtiers could think of little else but these 'privileges', as they were termed. The whole organization became like a school, with all its jealously guarded rights as to who may put his hands in his pockets or wear a certain scarf or hat. Certainly the men and women behaved like children and literally fought as well as bickered about the slightest right, as to who should stand here or there, how far forward or backward, who might perform this or that service for the king or queen, who had the right of entry to the different functions, who should give precedence to whom, and all the rest.

Here it is perhaps enough to outline a few of the fundamentals that concerned the reigning sovereign or his consort, since these lay at the root of all performances. At the strictest courts, notably Spain and France, virtually every action of the king or queen had to be attended by some officers in waiting, who had certain real or ritual observances to perform, with a noble chamberlain maintaining the rules.

In Spain the issue was so complicated that, on pain of death, the persons of their Majesties might not be touched by ordinary people, even in the event of an accident. Other courts were only a little less severe, and even tiny principalities had their insistences. Naturally a great deal depended on the nature of the prince and the scale and capacity of his court to play the game. But, however democratic some of them may have been, all princes were punctilious in following the accepted rules on state occasions.

Apart from the special mystico-religious rituals at great performances like coronations, funerals, weddings or the birth of an heir, which could, and did, fill volumes in themselves, the main daily performances concerned the sovereign's rising – the lever – his going to bed – the coucher – and the etiquettes at mealtimes.

These occasions are stressed for their formality, they stand apart from deferences at receptions, balls or the theatre, which were – or were supposed to be – for entertainment, and where the etiquettes were manners rather than court ritual.

At almost all courts the lever and coucher were the most significant. The highest household officers and ministers in office, and members of the royal family – male – entered the king's state bedchamber and there, according to the rules of that court, performed – in reality or symbolically – certain menial tasks for the king. Handing the shirt to Majesty was considered a great honour and might well be performed by the highest ranking prince or officer present, and so with lesser officers coping with minor tasks, the gloves or coat, orders or ruffles. At times the courtier might perform the whole service himself, but more often he would

merely pass the clothes or objects to the valet who actually helped His Majesty on with them. Carrying the king's candle was made a mark of considerable distinction at Versailles.

The significance attached to these formalized services was emphasized in the public beddings on wedding nights, when, in contrast, the king himself would often serve his eldest son. But that was about the only occasion when anyone thought to make anything of a joke of these performances. Attendance was the greatest honour and to be allowed to take an active part a privilege. All helped to stress the apartness of the prince. The practical,

Louis XIII, Anne of Austria and the Dauphin at the theatre with Cardinal Richelieu. By etiquette only the King and Queen have arms to their chairs; the Dauphin has one in miniature. Even the great Cardinal himself is only allowed a stool. The rest stand.

Above An English royal commode of the late 17th or 18th century upholstered in velvet. *Left* Design for a State bed for George I of England by John Vardy.

Improbable though it may seem to us, all these objects were the focus of formidable etiquettes in their time. Usually none was made use of by the king without one or more persons in formal attendance.

A 'cadenas' or napkin box bearing
the arms of William III of
England.

as opposed to the romantic or snobbish aspect of all this was that
it brought the courtier concerned into contact with the king, and
one never knew when an occasion might not arise to press some
case for profit. The coucher merely reversed the processes. The
fact that the king might not sleep in the state bed into which so
many tired people had put him, but, once the light was out, go
into a warmer room, or to a wife or mistress, was of no concern.
Nor indeed was the morning meeting disturbed by the fact that
many Majesties would have been up, dressed and washed (when
they did wash) by their personal valets and at work some time
before getting back into bed for the official lever. In courts where
official timing was kept absolute, such attendances, though boring
to all but the most enslaved sycophant, were at least predictable
and the courtier attending would generally know his hours. At
some, usually the lesser courts, the prince was often erratic and yet
expected that his little entourage should play the game, whether
at six, or eight or nine in the morning, or earlier, or not till midday
if His Highness had a hangover. That the household had been
literally 'waiting' for hours was regarded as their duty, privilege
and honour, the price they had to pay, or what they were there to
do. Similarly the coucher might be at any time in less disciplined
establishments. None the less, if the courtier wanted to be a courtier he was expected to play his part and wait up like the servants
until all hours if Majesty required. Consideration occasionally
came naturally to individual Highnesses, but it was far from being
universal as an attribute among absolutists.

The precedent for such procedures went far back. Kings had
always been attended and dressed by 'gentlemen' if not always
nobles. The many instructions are exact as to how those functions
should be carried out, as, indeed, they are indicative of the lapses
which must often have occurred. In the directives for those in
attendance on Henry VIII, it is recommended that 'gentlemen' in
attendance should be 'well languaged, expert in outward parts and
meet and able to be sent on familiar messages, or otherwise, to outward princes when the cause shall require'. This reads reasonably
enough, but other injunctions against slovenliness and undue
familiarity suggest that they were often rough, and not always
too clean or as fastidious about their persons as might be desirable.
It is interesting how centuries later, in all the plays, duennas or
characters like Mr Fagg, the young valet in *The Rivals,* combine
the same joint services of dresser and confidential messenger. He
was intimate, and in his case also saucy. For those who waited
upon royalty much of the same intimacy must have occured,
though not perhaps the sauciness.

Such a curious combination of personal service and intimacy
could be human as well as profitable and even held as an honour,

just as many a young lordling is happy to serve his prefect in traditional English public schools, without being insulted or dishonoured even if he has to take a beating into the bargain. Such, presumably, was always the attitude, but it is a far cry from 'Help me off with these boots, young man' or whatever the Viking equivalent may have been, to a ritual as serious as a mass and held to confer great honour on the highest in the land who might participate.

At other courts attendance at an actual rising may not have been included, but almost all monarchs held some early morning reception in the state apartments. Anybody who was summoned, or had access, was supposed to attend and, as the king or prince passed through, he might salute or question the courtier or receive his suits or introductions. Attendances were often numerous, ministers, courtiers and suppliants coming to meet each other as well as press their business on the king. Such levers still persist.

For the queens, rising and retiring were not such open or political affairs, though most held them in some form, and the ladies-in-waiting usually performed a ritual service, such as holding the basin or towel, the jewellery or fan.

Kings and queens, or ruling princes and princesses did not always 'live' together in the intimacy of twentieth-century bourgeois life. Usually each had a separate household and apartments at the palace. They often ate apart, dining alone in their own suites, when not in public state. At certain well organized times they would 'call' upon each other whether for sex or conversation. Evenings might be spent together, at an upon court or with a small group in private apartments. It is worthwhile to recall that apart from the most intimate moments, which seldom included the close stool, royalties were almost never, ever, quite alone; someone, noble or domestic was always 'in attendance' for protection or for company, while at night a guard, a valet or a maid slept in the same room or next door.

The second main focus of daily ritual at almost every court was mealtimes. On state occasions the ritual here could be fearsome, ranging from trumpet blasts or even cannon sounding every time a royal drank – with differing blasts for different ranks – through highly complicated standing or seating orders, to a mist of formalities as to who should carry what and give it to whom before it ever reached the royal lips or hands. At most of the larger courts the dish was finally presented by a nobleman (or woman for the queen) often on his knees. One overall principle seems to have been general: no one except royals of the immediate family or visiting princes ever ate at the same table or at the same time as the king or queen, even when each was dining alone in his or her apartments. At some courts it was not even allowed for princes

As it was not made in the 18th century, this vast rococo State bed from the Linderhof in Bavaria is perhaps even more impressively redolent of the rituals of the lever, which was one of the great basic formalities of absolutist power. Its splendour and magnificence were typical of the demands of the unhappy 'Mad' King Ludwig II of Bavaria, whose lack of inhibitions made him even more rococo than his 18th-century forbears in this field.
Implanted by his brutal 19th-century upbringing they led him to the outlet of architectural excess. Also perhaps he sought compensation against the new, more 'constitutional', approach of monarchy, to which he himself did not subscribe.

of the blood to eat with Majesty except on special occasions. At state banquets or on outside occasions, the exclusiveness might be modified and at some courts ambassadors, as representing other royalty, might be permitted to join in. This did not mean that courtiers were not expected to attend the process and to stand about till Majesty was finished, as we see in the painting by Paret. If the king dined alone, they might be called upon for conversation or questioning, to make arrangements for the afternoon or the next day's sport, and so on. At some courts the crown dined publicly, and anyone sufficiently well dressed could stand and watch.

These standing attendances at meals were dictated by the generally accepted ritual that none might sit before royalty. This particular distinction was everywhere maintained in one form or another. Normally, only the king and queen or very special princes or visiting royalty had armchairs. On formal occasions, like weddings of the crown prince, the royal children might be honoured with armchairs, though perhaps of a smaller size, in the presence of their parents. Princes and princesses of the blood might have seats with backs. In most cases the only others that might sit at all were ladies of the rank of duchess, and then only on stools. All the rest stood, and on really formal occasions did so for hours and hours on end. While strict formality of place and behaviour was enjoined by etiquette, in practice the people lolled about in pretty informal attitudes – the most informal being the favourite dogs which are spoken of in every palace, and often, feelingly, as ill house-trained.

Such rituals of precedences and of standing or seating were associated with every aspect of court life, from intimate attendance to the theatre or the street. On informal occasions some kings or queens might relax the rules for very favoured friends or visitors but only in the private apartments. Many kept the rules up everywhere, even in outside houses which they might deign to visit. Here, unless specially indicated, everyone stood all the time and normally the host or hostess had to serve.

All these performances were, of course, copied or followed in their own homes by princes of the blood, the greatest ministers and aristocrats, most of whom had levers and couchers of a sort.

Apart from these formalities there were also the rules of daily behaviour before royalty governing those fortunate enough to be presented or to gain access for a private audience. A bow, kneeling on one knee, or occasionally on both, were commonly expected, according to house rules. Others were axiomatic. Some of these, such as that of walking backwards over a polished floor gave great trouble to the inexperienced. Maria Theresa excused David Hume, the Scottish historian, when she saw him likely to fall. At

Since it affected personally everyone who came to court, the etiquette which virtually forbade anyone to sit before a royal must have been most widely effective. How many hundreds of people looked longingly at a stool like this one, which was made about 1840 for the Palace at Turin. On formal occasions only a duchess, at the very least, would normally have had the opportunity to use it for the purpose for which it was designed. Informally, certain royals would be more condescending, though by no means all.

private audiences, one bow at the door, one half way and another, or a genuflection, at the end, was regular.

Such general rules apart, the number of little rituals the courtiers and household thought up for themselves were endless, and most concerned their own privileges. Rituals for putting on or taking off the king's boots, rituals for handing the basin and towels after meals, rituals for poking the fire or possibly even taking the dogs for a walk; rituals for accompanying Majesty on travel, on horse, in the coach, on foot, hunting, or even on his close stool, were innumerable. They were jealously guarded and no one would perform another's function even – as was once reported in Spain – if the palace was likely to burn down as a result.

As an illustration of the ultimate in farce of such minutiae we have the story of the '*pour*' (for) at Compiègne. Louis XIV had arranged a vast review to which everyone was invited, including the ambassadors. These suddenly insisted that the word '*pour*' should precede their names, which were chalked upon the doors of rooms they were to occupy. This fuss was not new, and arose because a practice had grown up by which the princes of the blood might have this prefix on their doors. The ambassadors said that, as royal representatives, they too should have '*pour*' written on their doors. The king said this was nonsense and refused to give way or to concede such a precedent, although he was very anxious that his vast review should be observed by as many people as possible and especially the foreigners. The ambassadors remained intransigent and so they did not see the show. Few things better illustrate the importance attached to these formal etiquettes and practices, or the stupidity of the store people set by them. But as they served to stress the situation of the prince as standing at the apex of society, the motions were outward and visible signs of the spiritual mystique and power of monarchy.

Reasonably enough the greatest and most elaborate developments occurred on outstanding state occasions, such as coronations, official visits or marriages, when there was every excuse to make a maximum effort. Then the formalities were prodigious. Some details are outlined later, but the Schönbrunn illustrations give a vivid idea of what might be involved. When it is considered that every person in this vast cortège – except the simple soldiery – would be watching every move in relation to his or her own personal position in it, the effort can be appreciated. Working all this out took months before the marriage of Marie Antoinette, and covered every possible detail, from how the proclamation should be worded in order that each monarch should have his full respect and due, down to the ordering of the pages. The presentations, the receiving and the attendances, the introductions – everything had to conform to its allotted and decided pattern. Nothing was left to chance. Obviously with thousands of people parading in gala dress, some order had to be established, but the underlying interest was not so much an avoidance of chaos as the visible expression of the individual pomp and circumstance of those involved, and so a confirmation of the system as a whole.

Although the king, as absolute head, was bound by nothing, there were normal etiquettes, which virtually amounted to those of good manners, that the prince was expected to observe and that evolved a language all their own. If none wore a hat before him except by special licence he, in turn, might raise his own in salute as occasion called – particularly to ladies. The manner and degree of such a gesture like any other – whether extending his hand or bowing – was then capable of infinite variation to suit the circumstances and convey rebuke, indifference or approbation as the case might be. Every concession was a sign of approval and these were watched for by courtiers as the omens which indeed they were. An ambassador greeted before he had made his full quota of obeisance knew his case was sure.

If these royal gestures were not actually codified as were the more general performances, any and everyone knew every shade of their interpretation. As his tutor wrote to Prince Charles, later Charles I of England, '... Though you cannot put on too much *King*, yet even there, sometimes, a hat or a smile in the right place will advantage you'.

Similarly, gestures of courtesy and welcome to distinguished visitors, though never effusive, were a matter of grave significance. The formalities of these occasions could again fill books: how far and which royal carriages were sent; the state and number of the guards; the train of representatives; the nuances of meeting visitors, whether at the coach, the door, at the top of the stairs or in a state room, were all most carefully measured. The meeting of the Elector of Bavaria and the Archbishop of Salzburg described on page 149 gives some idea of what might be involved.

By making such rules and regulations for every aspect of royal life and its surroundings the mystique was aided and, incidentally, otherwise fruitless days given some further point, as time was passed in the extended theatrical ritual.

Princes of the Blood

The 18th-century world depended upon a handful of ruling people, who were, for the great part, selected by the chance of birth and from the outset were set apart and conditioned in a sense of their apartness and superiority. This ivory carving by J. C. L. von Lücke shows the heir presumptive to the Danish throne, Prince Frederick, born in 1753. Over his swaddling clothes he already carries the insignia of the Order of the Elephant, his country's most exalted Order, for which the greatest in the land would strive and even die. The two little princes shown on page 81 also carry their countries' highest distinctions, the Fleece and the Saint-Esprit. Such bestowing of honours, which may seem trivial to us, was all-important at the time and served to impress the mystique of royalty both on the young prince himself and on the world at large.

What chiefly concerns us in this chapter is the position of royal families as pawns in the political game, to which any of them could be sacrificed at any time. The emphasis on princes is deliberate, since the role of the princesses was so bound up with marriage that they are better discussed later with the queens.

If it was essential to the whole mystique that monarchy should be kept as remote as possible, it was no less prudent for any dynasty to have a pool of relatives in addition to the ruling prince himself. If it was highly desirable to have heirs for direct succession, it was also extremely valuable to have spare candidates ready to take advantage of any elective thrones or great ecclesiastical sees that might present themselves, or to acquire new lands by marriage. They might even be called upon to absorb some other principality or crown if the local family should die out.

This happened fairly frequently in smaller states but it could be of immense significance if larger nations were involved, as in the case of Spain at the death of Charles II, England at the death of Queen Anne, or the Grand Duchy of Tuscany on the death of the last direct Medici heir. In such circumstances, power politics played an all-important part and royal blood – in politically desirable veins – took precedence over any competence.

For princes awaiting such prizes, as for the majority to whom they never came, other roles had to be found. As brothers, sons, uncles or even cousins of the current Majesty they were kept about in greater or lesser state according to the local situation. They enhanced the palace ambience and formed a distinguished background. Occasionally they served as regents or as deputies or, if their relations with the crown were good, they might play an active part in armies or the conduct of affairs, though this was far from general. As history had shown, and still continued to suggest, royals could seldom wisely trust their nearest or dearest.

The history of monarchy is littered with attempts by sons or brothers, or even wives or mothers, going to any lengths to get the throne. At the beginning of the seventeenth century, Louis XIII had had any amount of trouble with his brother Gaston, and later even with his mother when her regency came to an end. Russian empresses of this period contrived or connived at the murder of

Even cradles had to emphasize greatness. This elaborate one was produced for the Duke of Bordeaux as late as 1820 by Rémond, Besnier and Matelin on a commission from the city of Paris.

sons or husbands with perfect equanimity – and very lucky it seems to have been for the country that they did.

The reverse could also happen as in the case of the aged Vittorio Amedeo, King of Sardinia, who abdicated in 1730 in favour of his son. Some said it was to allow him to devote more time to his mistress; others, more poetically, stated that he wished to allow himself an 'interval of retirement between the throne and the tomb'. Whatever the cause, the old gentleman soon repented of his generosity and robustly set about to remove his son and to regain his crown. The guards, however, decided to remain true to the young king, Vittorio Amedeo's attempt did not succeed and his son felt compelled to imprison his father (without the mistress, but with the usual accompaniment of tears and protestations about filial duty).

In practice, while it was essential for rulers to adhere to the principle of royal distinction, all had to be most careful that no member of the family with this inherited advantage should seek to profit by it before the time was ripe. It was considerations like these that governed the upbringing of royal children.

In education as in everything else under this system, the treatment of princes and princesses varied enormously with the personality of the monarch. In the larger and more severe courts the children tended to become part of the ritual from the day of their public birth or their public christening. They had their own 'household' of attendants, pages, servants, and nurses, wet or dry. In state cradles and stiff heavy clothes they started their passage to the grave in formal circumstance and etiquette. Family love or affection at this stage seems to have been rare and parental association would usually be limited to short visits. Mortality was high.

In some smaller courts, especially among the Germans, an easier situation might prevail and children would be brought up according to the current ideas of the upper classes. These were seldom very intimate and though some sentimental moments could occur, with mutual demonstrations of a parental love or filial duty, the system was based on the premise that children were better seen than heard, and not too often at that. In such circumstances, the nurses could play an important part in the forming of royal character, though no one was particularly aware of such psychological factors in the eighteenth century. True or not, the report is interesting that even the formidable Louis xiv used to be tucked up and kissed by his ancient nanny right up until her death.

By the schoolroom stage, at the age of three or four, governesses were introduced. Again, their influence could be considerable, and often the only warm association that many little princes or princesses ever knew was with their governess. Normally drawn from impoverished aristocracy or gentry, these ladies usually had

The infant Prince of the House of
Austria, later Emperor Charles VI
(top left), and the child Charles
Philippe, Comte d'Artois *(right)*,
both, as we have noted,
decorated with the most important
Orders of their lands. Equally
indicative of a prince's conditioning in apartness is the page from
the young Dauphin's copy book
(left), insistent in its repetition of
sentiments loyal to his dynasty,
so soon to be contradicted by the
guillotine.

A princely toy.

full control, and guarded their charges night and day. At other courts, some noblewoman might attend on state occasions, and was nominally in charge, while the actual nursery training and the day to day supervision was undertaken by a person of less rank. These might bring the children for formal presentation to their parents once or twice a day and supervise such play as there might be. Mostly princes and princesses only played with each other (if there were enough of them) or with carefully chosen little playmates of their own age. Here, human relationship and local availability might upon occasion, replace the formal principle, and boys and girls of fairly modest birth could be selected from the children of the household.

In the more domesticated courts the parents might begin to show some signs of affection at the schoolroom stage, treasure little gifts, worry about chicken pox (or, far more seriously, smallpox, which was rife), and listen to piping recitations from their brood.

At six or seven serious education had begun and at this point the more interested monarchs started to take part in what was going on, preparing notes and memoranda, especially in the case of the eldest sons. Others just did not want to know. At this stage boys were removed from governesses and placed in the hands of governors, whose business it was to supervise the growing up of the little royals. They too were usually, although not necessarily, of noble birth.

Work concentrated on deportment, behaviour, and such necessary accomplishments as arms or equitation. Dancing and music might be encouraged. The intellectual curriculum was seldom excessive and likely to be limited to languages and history, perhaps some politics and occasionally mathematics or some very elementary science.

For general subjects teachers were drawn from persons locally available, who tried as best they could, though for the greatest princelings scholars and tutors might be brought in from outside. The governor's business was rather to watch over the whole character formation of the boy and to see that he grew up along the paths of manners, manliness and courage, as well as knowing all the ritual and etiquettes of court.

These governor's requirements were admirably summed up by critics of the Maréchal de Villeroi when he was appointed governor to the boy king Louis xv. They confessed that he was a very proper person to teach the young monarch to walk, to put his hat on with a grace, to accost a lady in the politest manner, and other things of that nature; but that he was by no means fit to inspire him with ideas suitable to his rank – he would never make him 'think like a king'. Nevertheless, the narrator goes on to add that the marshal apparently had been successful in the latter since: 'Another day the French Comedians having played the tragedy of Athalia before His Majesty, 'tis said that the Prince could not bear with any patience to see young Joas seated on the throne, for he had a fancy he was a second king; nor would he so much as applaud the lad who had so perfectly played the part of Joas'.

In spite of all the surroundings of deference and respect the governors often had strong powers, and discipline was expected even from princes. Some, like Frederick the Great, suffered under a childhood of whippings that appeared excessive even in those stern times, though others were held so sacrosanct in their persons that 'whipping boys' were kept for them – little friends who had to bear the punishment for any misdemeanour that the high-born playmate might commit. The principle was designed on the grounds that any prince should be so sorry that his friend was punished for his fault that he would immediately feel contrite and not err again – an attitude revealing the gothic idealism that still permeated so many royal association. How far practice might fall short of such noble sentiments is another matter. From the tricks that some of them got up to, far more questionable reactions might have been aroused. But since not even the encyclopedists had yet read or thought in terms of our psychology the issue stayed uncomplicated.

There is no doubt that royal tutors held a position of great trust and influence. They seem usually to have been devoted to their charges and often their influence extended long after the school-room, sometimes for life. Cardinal Fleury, ex-tutor to Louis xv and later first minister and for years virtual ruler of France, is an example. It was even sinisterly suggested by his enemies that he had deliberately kept the boy backward so as to make the prince ever more dependent upon himself.

If heirs apparent had, according to some theories, to be taught to 'think like a king', some parents were careful to take precautions against the hazards of dynastic and family strife. The most nervous of these gave their boys almost no political education. Others educated the first born but provided alternative curricula for younger princes. Some even sought to keep a second brother back. The homosexuality of Monsieur, Louis xiv's brother, has been attributed to this; the preferences or exclusions that occurred in the schoolroom might well extend to later life. The case of Ferdinand ii dei Medici who shared his governance with his brothers is almost unique.

In general, such formal education as a prince or princess might receive would finish in their early teens. By this time some were married, others had at least obtained sufficient knowledge to enable them to carry on their learning should they wish. Certainly

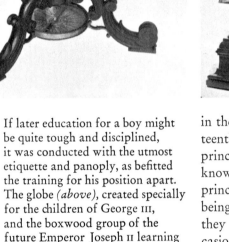

If later education for a boy might be quite tough and disciplined, it was conducted with the utmost etiquette and panoply, as befitted the training for his position apart. The globe *(above)*, created specially for the children of George III, and the boxwood group of the future Emperor Joseph II learning to ride both illustrate the princes' very special treatment.

in the seventeenth century, and even fairly generally in the eighteenth, academic abilities were not considered quite respectable in princes. Bishop Burnet, for instance, found Charles II's intimate knowledge of shipbuilding in excess of what was 'seemly' in a prince, and we often read of queens with intellectual leanings being at pains not to appear too learned. Further education – if they got it – was generally a matter of self development or, occasionally, for the boys, travel, or court or military experience.

It has already been stressed that the main purpose of those princes and princesses who were not the immediate heirs was in the dynastic marriage market, a value which could begin at puberty or even younger.

In the initial negotiations ambassadors reported confidentially on breeding prospects, comportment and the like, but apart from some interest in the former, the only considerations that really mattered were political. At the same time, in this paradoxical society a theatrical façade had to be maintained and as much play was made of love and beauty, as it was in any opera or novel of the day. Portraits and miniatures were exchanged, as well as presents that might – except perhaps, in value – be the tokens of a fairing shepherd.

Beauty and talent were always claimed, but the resulting partner, if not a mere child, was quite as likely to be a drunken huntsman as a model princely spouse, or, in place of the graceful beauty promised, an inhibited and rachitic skinflint, none too careful of her cleanliness or habits. Serene Highnesses did not take their choice, they took their luck. Lively reports were exchanged between relatives on the first meeting of the young couple, who

might never have seen each other before or even speak the same language, conclusions on the mating prospects were drawn from a smile or a frown, as if they had been dogs or cattle out at stud. Some suffered. Others saw it merely as the culmination of their early training and just another facet of apartness which made them so superior to the masses.

As may be imagined the actual marriage ceremonies and festivities were occasions of the greatest splendour, especially in the case of heirs apparent. Whatever dynastic or political issues were involved would be discreetly celebrated and the occasion used to make some contact with the general populace, who were encouraged to work up a fairy-story enthusiasm for the young couple, and afford them and the dynasty expressions of loyalty, which, it was hoped, would go on throughout their lives. Nor were the more intimate aspects of marriage forgotten, and public – if formal – 'bedding', after hours and hours of ceremonial and feasting, must have inhibited all but the most ardent lovers. Their conduct on this occasion was none the less a matter for more speculation, not to say ribaldry, among the higher intimates attending.

Against all this background of formality and detachment many baroque royals took their emotional – often sickeningly emotional – adolescent or adult family relationships very seriously. Both men and women were likely to blubber and cry on any moving occasion. Indeed it was regarded as a show of sensibility and feeling. In such circumstances it was only natural that any family misfortune should be an occasion for fine frenzy. Saint Simon draws a magnificently ludicrous picture of the Duke and Duchess of Bourgogne and the Duke and Duchess of Berri having a won-

Some works of art show the heir sharing with his father in the glory he is being fitted to assume. Joseph I is here seen in an ivory group by Daniel Maucher associated with the Emperor Leopold I in a triumph over enemies. The work shows also the kind of emotional sentimental attitudes that were a part of the period's reactions. Kind father strokes his darling son, while the latter looks adoringly at father. This public image took no account of the fact that, in many cases, father bullied son – if he paid him any attention at all – while the latter was scared stiff of his parents.

If childhood conditioning began at birth, results were expected very quickly and many royals were wedded in their early teens. This moving picture, attributed to Van Dyck, shows the boy Prince of Orange and his child wife Mary Stuart, daughter of Charles I. The seriousness of their little faces, the poise of stance and manner, the elaborate dress superbly worn, and even the protective delicacy with which he holds her hand, were what was expected of them.

derful public wake at the death of the dauphin, noisily weeping and crying, with the wives solicitously administering to their husbands. At least one of the party was delighted by the death, but joined in the theatre of misery as enthusiastically as the rest.

The most difficult situations were likely to occur as a result of differences between the parents and their children. The traditions of the time enjoined the most exact and classic filial obedience – another feature of the theatre extending into life. Having often neglected the children all their early days, these kings and princes, however, cynical of general loyalties, were for ever claiming parental love, filial obedience and filial piety, and then becoming hurt and tiresome if they did not get it. Even those who spoke to or referred to their children by their titles or in the third person, were none the less liable to throw themselves into screaming fits or turn on floods of sentimental tears if they did not get their way in issues where their children were concerned. The situation for the children was further exacerbated by the tradition of autocracy which also regarded them as subjects of their father, so that a double duty was owed. And then the family had an even further disadvantage of being always in the entourage and expected to behave as paragons. The result was often bitter. The first three English Georges hated their sons and heirs and never hesitated to say so.

If such deference and obedience came naturally to girls, or was so instilled that few princesses ever thought in other terms, it was often very difficult for any man or boy of spirit to endure. Many a prince's problems were complicated by an exhausting father-son relationship as he grew up. For heirs the situation might be yet more difficult, especially if they were born with aims and interests that were frustrated and denied expression.

No case was perhaps so complicated or disturbed as that of Frederick the Great and his relations with his father, Frederick William, who seems to have been a classic bully. The poor boy not only had to suffer inhuman discipline as a child, but the father continued publicly to humiliate and even beat the prince as a young man. The emotional tensions and the prince's acceptance of this handling (he would even weep in public for forgiveness at his father's knees) indicate the attitudes of the day, as well as the characters of the personalities involved. That Frederick William should totally ignore his son's tastes or wishes simply because he did not share them himself, might well be expected of any sovereign, but that he should dare to use extremes of emotional blackmail if there was the slightest resistence may be seen as human, albeit not humane. When, finally the young prince was driven to try to escape, the king had him arrested, imprisoned and court-martialled. Frederick William might have done anything, had not others intervened, since he had quickly blown up the whole affair into a plot against himself on the part of his son and his brother-in-law George of Hanover and England. Even so, although many thought the whole affair regrettable and shocking, no one questioned the king's right to take such action as he liked. Whatever the personal reactions and distress, when he eventually told his wife – the prince's mother – quite untruthfully – that the boy was dead, no one doubted that the king could well have ordered his son's execution with or without trial. This was his prerogative. As it was, in spite of the court-martial's recommendation of clemency, the king decided to execute the prince's friend and accomplice in flight, Von Katte, some say before the prince's eyes.

The extent and force of parental duty at another age can be seen in the relationship between Maria Theresa and Joseph, her co-regent son. She was religious, conservative and matriarchal, which put her into direct opposition to her son, who was an intellectual, near atheist, and almost revolutionary in his views. Inevitably they were in continual disagreement, but as long as she remained alive the empress had her way, getting it very often not by reason, though she was shrewd, but by using the most disgusting means of personal and moral blackmail about filial duty, the sorrowing, hurt mother, or any other emotional stop she could pull out.

A happier example of children used as successful pawns in the inter-royal power game is to be found in the sons of the Elector Max Emanuel of Bavaria. Although the elector had not always succeeded in his military commitments he certainly saw to it that his sons both earned their keep and contributed to serving the family cause. One, Karl Albrecht, managed for a short time to be elected Holy Roman Emperor, one of the rare occasions when this prize was wrested from the Hapsburg claim.

But perhaps the most spectacular career was that of the fourth son, Clemens August. Briefly, his biography runs thus: born in 1700, he was destined from an early age to represent the family's interests in the valuable field of ecclesiastical might and power. Max Emanuel had been defeated in the War of Spanish Succession, but recovered quickly, and by 1718 the young Clemens August had been made Abbot of Altötting, an important charge which might serve to get his hand in. The next year timely deaths and family pressures saw him elected Bishop of Münster and Paderborn. By 1723 he was Elector and Archbishop of Cologne, a great electoral see with vast wealth and influence, to which posts he added, in the following year the Bishopric of Hildesheim. At this point it was thought desirable that he should take Holy Orders, which he did in 1725 at the age of twenty-five; two years later, he received his bishop's investiture at the hands of the pope.

Nothing could convey better than these three portraits the superlative sense of apartness and dignity which childhood conditioning and education were designed to create in an 18th-century prince. Above right is the full figure of the life-size silver votive statuette of the young Prince Maximilian Joseph of Bavaria, executed by Willem de Groff in 1737. The superbly insolent portrait by Louis Toque (*above*) shows the young Pfalzgraf Friedrich Michael von Zweibrücken Birkenfeld, while the brilliant lead bust by F. X. Messerschmidt (*left*) carries all the dignity of the Imperial house in the handsome features of this proud prince of Austria.

In all this Clemens August's own participation may have been small, but family machinations had succeeded in making of this young man one of the wealthiest and most influential potentates of Europe – not bad going for someone who, though not a fool, and of great taste in art and hunting, had tendencies to melancholia. His really outstanding qualification, in the terms of the day, was that he was the son of his father, with the right quarterings and background. Even the most notable dynastic heritages of industrial or newspaper magnitude today, pale before such an accretion of honours and titles, with the accompanying rents and power, on the part of a younger son. When, shortly after, at the age of thirty-two, he was nominated High Master of the Teutonic Order his position linked him with almost every noble, crowned and princely family east of the Rhine. He used the profits from his various positions to become one of the most tasteful builders of his age, spending astronomical sums on several palaces.

While the story of Clemens August is exceptional, the principle of exploiting sons and daughters to the best advantage went on everywhere in Europe, on whatever scale the pretendants could manage or afford. Often sheer luck, or some arrangement to avoid a clash of conflicting candidates, might settle the day. The selection of Maria Leczynska, daughter of the impoverished Stanislas, ousted king of Poland, to be the wife of Louis xv, was an example, if an unusual one, since Stanislas, though ex-elected king, was not of royal descent by birth. For this match, local Versailles intrigues, to gain their own ends, were entirely responsible.

To return from the particular to the general, most princes by their late teens were set up in their own palaces or houses with a pension, household and gentlemen, if they had not already acquired these earlier on marriage. This did not mean that they were absolved from attendance at the court or from waiting on their sovereign. The poorer ones often sought military appointments, either at home or abroad, if they had any leaning for that exercise. Sometimes, richer or more enterprising monarchs sent their sons on tour, usually incognito (as Count this or that). This anonymity served a double purpose in that royal cousins, who were still expected to receive them, were saved the trouble and expense of formal inter-royal hospitality, while at the same time any youthful peccadillos could be more easily overlooked.

It was when grown up and married and beginning to settle down that the prince's chances of happiness or frustration might come to a head, for there was little freedom, and at all times life and daily conduct depended from the sovereign's order. In the case of heirs apparent they could at least look forward to eventual heritage, but more distant brothers, uncles, cousins, as also aunts and nieces, were entirely at the sovereign's whim. If relations were fairly close and cordial, as between the brothers Frederick and Henry of Prussia, or Leopold of Tuscany and Joseph ii, the younger brother might work out a full and interesting life, participating in affairs and helping king and dynasty. Some were trusted – often disastrously – with military commands and a few with local governorships and similar posts. If – as was often the case – relations were not good, then the situation could be difficult indeed, for both tradition and practical politics demanded that all the immediate family should be at court, if only to keep them under surveillance. As their rank and etiquettes forbade any intimate associations, beyond mistresses, outside the restricted family circle, they were thrown back on each other day after day, week after week, whether love or hate dictated the relationship. It was virtually house arrest and if they did not like their gaoler it was harsh. At least they were generally as well maintained as family finance would allow, if only because it did not help the mystique for a royal to go in rags.

For those who were content simply to be a prince of the blood and play at nothing more than court and entertainment, hunting, gambling, dressing, theatre and the rest, the circumstances were

For royal children even the fonts might be special and made of the most costly material and exquisite workmanship. This plate shows the silver font of the royal family of Sweden, made in Stockholm between 1697 and 1707 by a French goldsmith, François Cousinet, invited by Charles ix.

good. At least they could be leaders in court affairs and gossip, dance attendance and collect their Orders like the rest. It is not to be imagined for a moment that these princes thought themselves above such baubles; on the contrary they scrambled for them with the best. Sometimes they would try to hold a lesser, independent court, with a different style of company or easier circumstances, but there was always the danger of the sovereign's jealousy. If this was made apparent, their entourage would melt away. Every diary expands upon the fickleness of those who waited on the heirs, the mistresses and ministers. There was a tight-rope to be walked as between personal preference and career: the insurance policy element in over- or under-estimating the life span of incumbents as against the chances of an heir apparent. In an absolutist court it was manifestly dangerous to back an unpopular child. Even in England, the Georges did their utmost to exclude from court anyone who followed their wayward sons. In Britain they could do little more, but elsewhere, banishment or prison were of easy access to the king and could be used to serve his purpose at the slightest whim.

For princesses the controls were stricter and they stayed at home. For those unmarried, things could well be harsh. Morganatic marriages were not considered and for those whose chances of a royal mate were finished nothing but the convent or an undesired old maidhood were allowed. A few had the money and permission to set up elsewhere on their own – but this was far from usual. The unhappy daughters of George III called Windsor their nunnery – which indeed it may well have resembled after the king went mad, and his queen, their mother, became soured by events and their beloved Regent brother kept away.

The case of bastards varied but, in general, their position declined in the eighteenth century. Seventeenth-century monarchs like Louis XIV or Charles II accepted theirs – or some of them, the former even seeking to have his favourites, the Duc du Maine and M. de Toulouse, who had been officially 'legitimated', put in line for the succession. But no sooner was he dead than the other 'princes of the blood' rallied round to get the act rescinded. Compromise was reached, after a long unseemly wrangle, and it was finally agreed among the family that, though 'legitimated' princes should continue to enjoy the rank of 'princes of the blood' for life, neither they nor their heirs could follow to the throne.

By the eighteenth century even acceptance had become more rare. The exceptional bastard might rise to be a general, but usually a title and emoluments were the limits of possibility, and these only to sons of favoured mistresses of noble birth.

Detail of the life-size silver votive figure of the young Prince Maximilian Joseph (the whole is shown on p. 89) presented to the church of Altötting on the occasion of the prince's recovery from a dangerous illness. Here is real fairy-story distinction, beauty, wealth and exclusivity.
The mixture of extravagance, sentimentality, religious subscription, family pride and dynastic superbia which went into the commissioning of this lovely work of art are so intermingled that it would be impossible to say which contributed more powerfully to its creation.

Queens and Princesses

In his painted wooden figure of the royal St Kunigunda, from the church at Rott am Inn, the great carver Ignaz Günther has given us the 18th century's ideal of a queen. The superlative aloofness, beauty, elegance and distinction with which she has been endowed was what everyone looked for. Born and conditioned to great position, queens were beings apart. Some even believed that royals could only breed through them, an illusion usually quickly shattered on marriage. Their apartness has seldom been more effectively expressed than by the Beatle, John Lennon, when, in a recent interview, speaking of Elizabeth II, he said simply 'but I am sure the Queen must think she's different.' Perhaps, for newer worlds, where even the proper significance of the word 'gentleman' is not understood, a full conception of royal apartness cannot really be conveyed.

In this chapter a distinction has to be made between queens as heads of state in their own right, and queens as the wives of kings. It is with the latter that we are chiefly concerned, if only because the former were so similar, in their actions and reactions, to their male counterparts, that there is little reason to look further — though it might be that their sex gave them some advantages in this unscrupulous game, through those last elements of gothic courtoisie which still allowed a woman some slight edge. The Emperor Joseph II, speaking to the British ambassador about Catherine the Great, opined that 'whoever has to deal with her must never lose sight of her sex, nor forget that a woman sees differently from our sex'. After this resounding platitude he continued that it was necessary to 'give her her way in matters of little consequence, to render every necessary refusal as palatable as possible, to let her perceive a constant desire for pleasing', and very much more in the same vein. Poor Joseph, no one should have known better, since his mother's femininity certainly gave him frustrations enough during the period of their co-regency. Had he read Catherine's patronizing assessment of himself he might have felt less tolerant: 'The right noble apprentice has far to go yet before he can become a journeyman ... It is said that he thinks well; that is possible, but one can also say that of a goose.'

The case of Queen Christina of Sweden, her conversion and abdication, poses curious psychological problems, which history may not, as yet, have answered completely, but other queens, like Anne of England, Maria Theresa of Austria and the Empresses Elizabeth and Catherine of Russia ruled as men, nor did they do at all badly. Queen Anne, dull though she was, managed her ministers and government with all the Stuart determination to get her own way. Indeed, she has been accounted the last real autocrat of England, perhaps again because her feminine unreasonableness received the same romantic deference from men. In the intervals of rule, Anne was domestic enough to breed copiously from her sot of a husband, though all the children died early. But she was as much at the mercy of her favourites, like Sarah Churchill or Mrs Masham, as had been the first of the English Stuarts. Apart from that, she was comfortable, with flashes of commen sense; she

95

Unhappily for princes, queens in real life were not always like those of fairy story. Neither the redoubtable amazon Duchess of Parma *(left)* nor – if her wax effigy from Westminster Abbey is to be credited with any likeness – Her Grace of Richmond *(right)* would be likely to draw a crowd if presented on an ordinary stage today.

did no better nor worse than the average of her royal contemporaries, or most of the twentieth century's presidents or ministers.

Maria Theresa was basically a conservative, formidable, matriarchal noblewoman, who could have well performed the task of ruling any manor. She was shrewd, with perhaps a more than masculine obstinacy and determination, and was obsessed with the dignity of the House of Austria. If she got what she wanted she was agreeable, and she also managed to combine a fairly homely and democratic way of life both in private and in public with extravagantly elaborate official functions, when she could be prodigal, especially in the early days. She shared the throne first with her husband and then with her far more able son. The arrangement was perhaps a complicated mixture of family sentimentality and desire for male support. It also retained the elective Roman Imperial title in the family, and made a nice conformist gesture to the ideal of the obedient woman deferring to her men. Nevertheless, she saw to it that she got her own way and was not above using the most sickening moral blackmail to do so.

At least in the case of Maria Theresa and Queen Anne no one could have questioned their adherence to traditional family

Somewhere between the ideal and its opposite comes the homely figure of the Empress Maria Theresa. The medium of Capodimonte porcelain has rendered a rather sympathetic portrait and conveys some feeling of robust femininity, though it does not present a woman with whom anyone would be likely to take liberties. This was probably a very good likeness of the Empress.

morality. In this they differed from two notable Russian Empresses Elizabeth and Catherine. These two behaved exactly as the more emancipated monarchs of their time, though Catherine could come over all girlish and send little notes to her stalwart bedfellows. Such rather elephantine tendernesses seem comically operatic in a woman of her brilliance and cynicism, whose rise to the throne was quite ruthlessly – if justifiably – arranged through her husband's murder.

For queens by marriage, life might be a very different affair. Existing in a man's world mainly by virtue of their husband's position, what they thought or what they did was largely a result of the contact between the two personalities. Some had loving and successful lives, and their husbands openly pined when they died; some were neglected and unhappy; some dominated, others were doormats; some tried to play an active role in rule and politics, others were content to play a passive wifely part. In any case there seems to have been one thing common to the education of all of them, the principle of deference to their husbands. As in mediaeval times, the man was expected to be the head of the family and the wife look after him according to his wishes. Almost all diaries and correspondence emphasize this attitude as that expected of a royal as much as any other spouse. Most, at least at the outset, seem to have sought rather passionately to be good wives, obedient to their husbands and anxious to please them in every way, like the Queen of Saxony of whom it was written 'she is inviolably attached to her duties, full of tenderness and respect for her husband, and always wisely employed in what may procure his solid comfort'. This is certainly a nice 'slippers before the fire' approach, but marked examples of deliberate early unwifelyness and selfishness are rare; perhaps since so many were married as children, such docility is to be expected. Besides, they had their rank to think of. Certainly when Marguerite Louise d'Orléans sought to leave Cosimo dei Medici, who might justifiably have been regarded as anything but an ideal spouse (in part perhaps, because of her), and wrote to Louis XIV suggesting retirement to a convent in France, Louis roundly told her that any princess of France who left her husband and returned to France went to the Bastille and not to a convent.

In any event, a queen's position was one for which she had been bred and educated, an education which made no pretence at being much more than a conditioning for the station which it was hoped she would eventually hold.

As with the boys, the early stages of a royal lady's life might vary considerably according to the attitude of the parents, but this was rather in matters of detail than of fundamentals. Boys and girls always started off together in the nursery, and after the nursery came the schoolroom and governesses. At six or seven the boys were hived off, but the princesses' upbringing tended to persist in the governess tradition, with possibly a more developed interest in decorum, behaviour, and the etiquettes they were expected to observe. They were likely to have more contact with their parents at this stage and might even be taken up officially in some degree if their sovereign father liked to have his family around him. Only at the rarest courts was any display of intellect encouraged. Languages were thought important if only to equip the princess at the earliest age as a potential bride for a foreign husband. Dancing, deportment, music, genealogy and equitation were included on their curriculum.

The moment and degree of such participation in public events as was accorded to a princess was a matter for royal choice. Some kept their daughters away, others, like George III of England, liked to have them all around them – and very boring many people found it. Normally betrothal or the later teens was thought soon enough to enter public life; younger princesses kept to their apartments, mixing only with their family and relatives, or permitted friends. These latter seem not always to have been taken

Nearly approaching the unattainable ideal, at least in grace and charm, is the individual portrayed in Van Loo's painting from Versailles – Maria Leczynska, Polish wife of Louis XV of France. Certainly the clothes and settings of the time offered every opportunity, even if few were in a position to make much of it.

from the aristocracy; in the smaller courts they might, as with the boys, be drawn from children of the household.

Even in later years this taste for fairly intimate association with some member of the middle or the lower classes was a human feature with many royals. A number of reasons are obvious; if the contact occured at all it probably did so because of natural sympathy of temperament; there was also the possibility, if not the probability, that those so honoured might be less 'interested' and less likely to intrigue than the general attendance of the court. Furthermore there was some freshness of approach and perhaps, that sense of detachment which makes so many people gossip with their hairdressers and barmen. Marie Antoinette's association with Rose Bertin the couturière was an example. We are told how Rose, although a protegée of the Duchess of Chartres, was forbidden to attend the lever of the queen because her lack of rank denied this access even though the queen desired it. Yet she was allowed far more intimate attendance on Her Majesty in private when they could chatter and gossip as they wished.

Obviously in smaller courts such contacts would be far more readily accessible and just as a huntsman or gardener might become a friend of the prince by virtue of their close association and mutual interest, so many women must have sought for a change of face. Many were far too exigent or snobbish, but others were less demanding – or more bored with their restrictions.

Above As an illustration of the enormous train and elaboration which attended the marriage procession of a future queen, this night scene by Antonio Stom showing the arrival of Princess Amalia of Saxony is most effective.

Opposite From Palermo to St Petersburg – as here in the grounds of Tsarskoe Selo Palace – from Madrid to Munich or Stockholm, the chinoiserie fashion was expressed in play houses in an imagined Chinese taste. They often had two or even three floors and, like this one, could serve for quite numerous party guests even though they looked flimsy – an impression countered by the number of them still standing. Their popularity lasted throughout the 18th century.

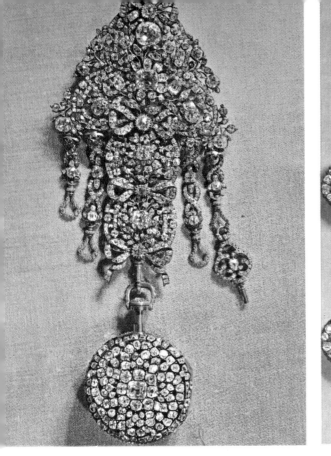

The eighteenth century tended to be less rumbustious in the upbringing of its royal girls than was the seventeenth, reflecting the general refinement of all manners and behaviour. Although hunting and even shooting continued to be permitted, the majority of princesses spent a great deal of their time at maidenly pursuits such as painting and embroidery, music, walking, or a limited and censored reading. A few became stalwart in the hunting field, on horse or in a calèche, but by and large eighteenth-century female royals contented themselves with rather silly games like Blind Man's Buff or Main Chaud on picnics and such similar diversions. For the rest, religious exercize (according to the court), occasional 'good works', discoursing platitudes and dressing up served to pass the day until the evening parties, balls or theatre.

In spite of the restrictions of society some managed to obtain a wide and often cynical approach to life. The letters of Wilhelmina of Prussia are not lacking in informed remarks, while the Demoiselles de France of Louis XV were, it is said, quite prepared to tell their father that he ought to get a mistress and so leave their mother less engaged – advice he took. The period attitude allowed for far more robust reference and conversation for either sex than in the nineteenth century.

Once grown up things might be sad indeed if they were not married. In this man's world there was little they could do. Marriage anywhere outside the circle was not envisaged, lovers really frowned upon, which virtually meant that any male friendship, however platonic, was unlikely to flourish. In later years the only acceptable alternatives were a rather distant, formal shelf, often on limited means, or good works or the convent. Not all the last were severe and at some, which were set aside for royals and aristocracy, receiving and even dances might find a place, as Queen Charlotte told Miss Burney. Many royal nuns lived happily; freed from the artificial life of court, they pursued their course with as much austerity as they might wish, or sometimes, in the case of those with a taste for power, became abbesses.

All such activities were, of course, but palliatives should the main purpose of a royal maiden not be fulfilled – that of marriage to an heir or to another prince of royal blood. Catherine the Great's reiteration in her memoirs of how she dreamed of being a great queen rings true; it was an attitude no doubt nurtured in the schoolrooms of most palaces and castles of those born to royal estate. However poor they might be – and among the lesser houses many even lacked linen and amenities – the fairy prince was always a possibility, and a pleasanter matter for contemplation than the convent or the shelf. The fairy-tales which tell of such events were more likely to be fare for palace nurseries than cottages or hovels.

When great matches did occur it was an occasion for pageantry and feasting for the world whatever the bride and the bridegroom might think. As far as these two were concerned it was usually an issue of obedience to family and dynastic ends.

As an illustration, the story of the wedding of Marie Antoinette and the Dauphin Louis (XVI) can scarcely be bettered. As we shall see when treating of ambassadors, the reasons for the marriage were political, but, once the political decision had been made, the negotiations dragged on for months and months. The negotiations were almost entirely to regularize minutiae of protocol and formalities concerned with the various festivities. The grown-ups wore themselves to shreds, but the child protagonists, he sixteen, she fifteen, were not consulted, though no doubt from time to time informed of what was going to be expected of them. So that at least they might have some (flattering) idea of each other, portraits and miniatures were exchanged.

Finally on 21 April 1769, after a week of formal balls and entertainment for the grown-ups, the girl of fifteen set out in a train of nearly sixty carriages, needing some four hundred horses, which had to be changed in relays throughout the day. The suite of some one hundred and fifty attendants ranged from two princes and a noble guard to cooks and washerwomen.

Travel might be for six or nine hours each day over the indifferent roads and every evening stop involved a party with relations or an official welcome. Church bells were rung along the route with all the populace turning out to watch the convoy. As Maria Theresa's court had been fairly loving and informal for the children, the princess must have had much to ponder along the jolting miles. After a formal welcome at the border by more grown-ups (parading more for their own interest and self-importance than hers), Marie Antoinette was taken into a specially constructed house. Here, on one side, open to Austria, she took leave of her Austrian suite. She was re-clothed, and passed through a door – into France. The princess had become French and was now presented with her French household, which was to number hundreds. A moment of childish reaction prompted her to embrace her new French duchess chief of household, but such demonstrations were not envisaged by the protocol and the other noble ladies of her train were more becomingly received.

Apart from this regrettable lapse, the child apparently behaved with perfect decorum, smiled everywhere and remained untired – or did not show it. She pursued her triumphal journey across France, with ever increasing receptions, ballets, theatres and balls until she met her father-in-law, his court and her sulky fiancé at Compiègne. At this stage the father-in-law at least was most impressed – more so than his son. The ageing Mesdemoiselles de

In writing about historical facts or stories concerned with royalty, it is very easy to underestimate the great significance of the sentiment of loyalty to the crown, which played an all-important part in government right up, indeed, until the present century and throughout almost all the world. On very rare occasions absolute rulers might be made the scapegoats for unhappiness, as came about in the case of Louis XVI and Marie Antoinette, whose marriage was recorded in this charming biscuit group by Lochre. A sacrifice such as theirs was rare, and the commonplace sentiments were just those recorded in this group, entitled *Hymen and the Genius of France*, made in 1774 to celebrate the wedding of the princely children.

A gilt bronze portrait of Marie Antoinette.

France, Louis' sisters, were not displeased and so the procession continued well. Even Mme la Comtesse du Barry, the king's current mistress (who, to the dismay of many, had been included in the reception line), found her charming. Narratives of the success were sent post-haste to mother in Vienna. Because the grown-ups were pleased with this charade of 'love' the child was held to have done her duty and maintained the honour of her house. No one could foresee that she was to do it even more impressively twenty years later on the scaffold.

Then came more formalities, receptions, the inevitable operas, theatres, ballets, parties and fireworks surrounding the actual marriage itself, which was conducted with extravagant ceremony. The cost was prodigious.

The circumstances of the First Lady of France might be expected to be exceptional, but any ruling house would have attempted such a display to the limit of its resources, or such credit as it had. These dynastic alliances were of such significance politically and as propaganda that nothing but the best would serve. The whole was always cloaked with allegories of love at every turn; with cooing doves and lovers' knots, arrows and hearts, entwined initials and all the paraphernalia of tender passion that was fitting for the operatic make-believe of court procedure. What the children did about it was another affair. After marriage and public bedding, poor Louis-August preferred sleep (and, we are told, he snored) to the pleasures of matrimony in preparation for which all this time and money had been spent.

In fact the poor boy suffered from a painful physical disability, directly concerned with the marriage bed, which was to develop psychological as well as physical disturbances both in himself and in his frustrated young wife. Had Louis-August been able to act normally in these early years perhaps Marie Antoinette would not have developed the extravagant frivolities associated with her.

If this reads like cruelty to children, a classic example of the extremity of cynicism for more adult royal marriages is offered by the circumstances surrounding the second marriage of James, Duke of York, later, for a very short time, James II of England. During his exile in Holland James had had an affair with – inter alia – Anne Hyde, a daughter of the Earl of Clarendon. She became pregnant and, rather curiously, his brother Charles (later Charles II) insisted, as the head of family, that James should marry this mistress despite their mother's loud insistence that she was of insufficient birth to marry her royal son. Anne died and James decided to marry again, for obvious dynastic reasons. Following the Restoration, James had become increasingly and avowedly Catholic. Internally, political opponents made such capital as they could out of this, while externally it afforded a great opportunity for attempts by the church and the European Catholic alignment to try and regain Britain for the faith. Louis xiv, whose policy had long upheld Charles ii, was directly interested. A Catholic marriage was important.

Ambassadors were alerted and various potential candidates reviewed. The report on one – a widow – included the assessment that 'If the duke desires a wife in order to have children he cannot do better than marry Mme de Guise, who has been with child three times in two years, and whose birth, wealth and prospects of fecundity, appear to me to atone for her lack of beauty'. Nevertheless the English envoy found her so unattractive that the suggestion was not further mooted. Some Germans passed into review, but finally the candidates were whittled down to two princesses from Modena, an aunt and niece. The latter, Maria Beatrice, 'Mary of Modena', won, though not without some dithering between the two. The aunt's retirement to a convent and the direct intervention of the pope settled the issue. The pope wrote personally to this child of fourteen years, intimating that she could do much more for Holy Church by marriage than by entering the cloister; this, far more than the urgings of her parents or relations, or even Louis, seems to have won the day. After endless commotions and tears the child set off with her mother, after a marriage by proxy in Modena. After a trying journey she finally reached London, fell for her brother-in-law, aroused a certain amount of political trouble, but soon fell in love with her husband, to whom she remained constantly devoted.

In practice, the greater number of such dynastic marriages worked out satisfactorily, as indeed with arranged marriages wherever the custom is accepted. Some wives became devoted, some just carried out their official role, a few made trouble, but almost none divorced or separated. After all they were women and most seem to have liked a man. With discrimination against morganatic marriages and polyandry a royal man was all they could hope for, so that it was only sensible to try and make the best of what they had, and that was what they had been trained to do. In any event, freedom of choice for women was not a generally accepted idea. Furthermore, marriage generally brought an advance of status, a detail about which gradations of Highnesses were as acutely conscious as any in the social rat race. They had that station which God had ordained for them and a sense of right and duty done for their House, if not always for themselves.

In such royal marriages, chastity was normally regarded as imperative for the bride just as premarital experience, unless very young, and postmarital infidelity were to be presumed among most grooms. If a mistress was too clearly flaunted too early, or the husband positively rude and cruel from the outset, relatives might

interfere. Otherwise, things took their course in a society permissive to the sufficiently privileged male.

Some marriages, like that of George III of England and Queen Charlotte, appeared as a model of domestic life, as far as the king and queen were concerned, at least to start with. They were obviously devoted to each other, though it is not to be imagined that fairly formal court etiquettes were allowed to lapse even with this very unassuming pair. The queen rose and curtseyed when the king came in and their conversation was properly sprinkled with 'Your Majesty'.

Not all royal marriages were as satisfactory and idyllic as the picture presented by George and Charlotte. Often there was a direct clash of personalities which – at least in smaller and more intimate courts – might find explosive outlet. In most cases the size of the establishments, as indeed the etiquettes and general traditions, allowed each to live almost entirely apart should they so wish, meeting only for formal functions when they would be expected to play their parts as king and queen, or prince and princess, rather than as husband and wife. Sense of position and family pride were the basis of royal as well as of lesser society, so that it was not too difficult to put on a sufficient show. Outside official hours the men could work or disport as they wished, but the women's opportunities were more restricted. In case of discord, or even lapses of an interest which may never have existed very keenly, the men could take their mistresses. Such activities were not allowed to queens and seem but rarely to have been indulged, possibly as much from reasons of snobbery as morality or Christian precept. If found out, prison for the queen and a nasty death for the lover were virtually inevitable unless the prince were too bewildered or too accommodating to care. George IV of England and the Grand Duke Peter were cases in point. The real grudge against Queen Caroline was that she had acted in a manner unbecoming to the monarch's consort, not that she might have committed adultery. Caroline in fact behaved very badly indeed and, whatever the justification, went to considerable pains to embarrass her husband, in which she was ably seconded by his political opponents. Justified or not, such wrangles were no particular advertisement for monarchy.

Occasionally human temperament overcame the veneer of royal upbringing; some took exception to their husbands' mistresses and were just plain jealous. It is a marked feature of eighteenth-century behaviour that most people reacted in the way they had been brought up to react, instead of attempting ratiocination in the manner of the Age of Enlightenment. It was enough for them to feel they ought to make a fuss for them to do so. Again we cannot overemphasize the tendency to artificial sentimentality in late

In this porcelain figure *(opposite)* a Dresden modeller has contrived to give something of human femininity to one of the most formidable women of her day, Catherine the Great. This was, perhaps, how she would have liked to be seen by the masses. Those at closer quarters might have other experience. The Empress' exquisite desk *(above)* shows another aspect of her remarkable and all-embracing taste.

eighteenth-century court life. Queen Victoria was the heiress, not the originator, of many attitudes attributed to her.

Also it may be suspected, whether the queen herself registered any particular sentiment or not, the court writers and gossips would attribute to her such reactions as were conventionally proper to the occasion. We are, for example, continually told how sad Maria Leczynska was made by her husband's infidelities. We are given a picture of the lonely queen sitting, hour after hour, weeping into her netting. This tallies badly with her other recorded comments, about receiving too much attention and living a life of nothing but bedding, pregnancies, births and then more bedding. She was treated with deference in court and one strongly suspects that she would never have accepted Mme de Pompadour as Dame d'Honneur if she had really hated her. Louis XV may have been superlatively selfish but he does not seem to have been so vindictive a cad as to force something unnecessarily unpleasant upon the queen.

Such reticence was not always the lot of all wives who were really disliked. Some met with indifference, but others, like the unfortunate queen who was put between Elector Johann Georg of Saxony and his mistress, might be subjected to physical violence as much as any other less exalted housewife. It is recounted that on at least one occasion she had to be rescued by the sheer brute strength of her brother-in-law.

The situation could happen in reverse, as with the hysterical and ill-natured queen of Prussia, of whom it is related that she rushed into her husband's room in her white nightdress screaming with rage, and cutting herself on the door she battered on. The vision so frightened the poor king that he retired to bed and shortly died of heart failure. He thought he had been visited by the family banshee which was alleged to make such an appearance before a death in the family.

Private relationships apart, an important issue might arise in the case of those queens whose ambition took them outside the narrow paths of court, parties or the etiquettes. An interest in politics was officially discouraged, but could be the natural result of boredom or a native instinct for power. One of the difficulties that all monarchs had to guard against was that their wives, inevitably drawn from some foreign power, might instinctively side with parents or relations abroad rather than with the country to which they had been sent. Here, although wifely tradition and indeed instruction made it clear that their duty lay to their husband, practice, especially in the less happy unions, often dictated otherwise. Some even became spies for parents, brothers or nephews, or even if the queen herself did not take an active part in this there was always the danger that members of her household might be used to such

Two souvenirs of perhaps the most romantic queen of the period, Marie Antoinette: a reconstruction of the famous 'Queen's necklace' *(above)*, a stupendously expensive jewel given or not given by an aspiring lover, and *(below)* her dog's extremely exquisite kennel made by the *ebéniste* Sené.

Popular enthusiasm for the royal family could be extended by prints such as this, issued for the wedding of Louis and Marie Antoinette in 1774.

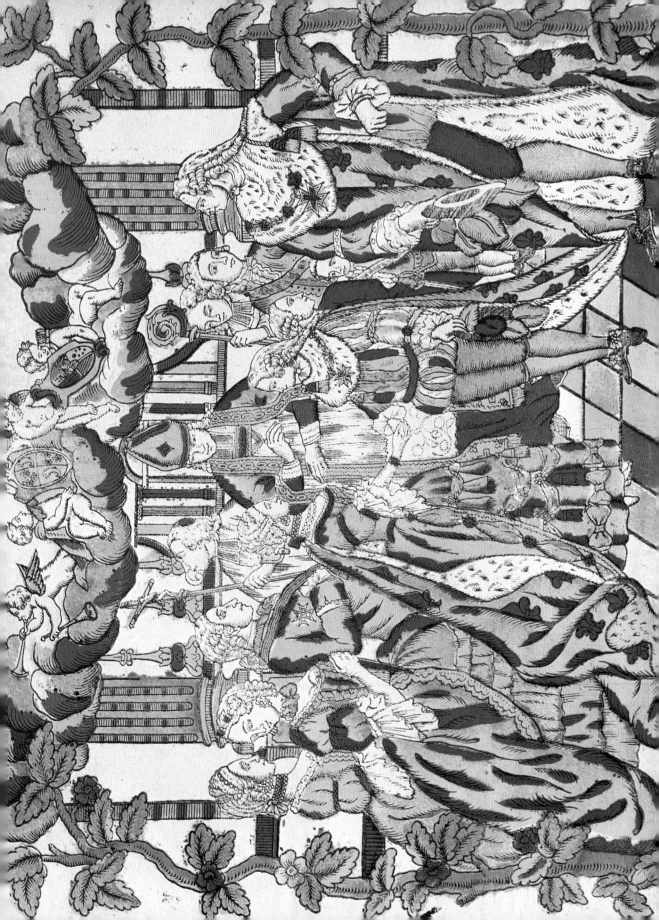

an end. For this reason newly arrived princesses were often allowed to keep only one or two minor servants from home within their entourage, and locally recruited persons of reliable political opinions were appointed to their household.

More important, perhaps, in the political field was the degree to which the queens might be able to influence their almighty men. This they shared with the mistresses, though on the whole perhaps less effectively. But, according to the circumstances, the queen's influence could be very powerful indeed. In the case of the queen to Philip v of Spain, it is alleged that she actually ran the country, seeking to have her way at every turn. If Richelieu is to be believed – which is not always the case – on the rare occasions when the king refused to do her bidding, Her Majesty would feed him aphrodisiacs and then refuse cooperation. As he was intensely devout and active, and did not allow himself the usual royal alternative, he was quickly brought to heel. Even with this determined lady the story emphasizes that she was at great pains to make it appear that everything emanated from the king and to let him think he was doing it all by himself. Like the ministers of the Emperor Charles vi, she gave the monarch an infinitude of little things to do to occupy his time while she conducted the real business of the country.

Others were less dramatic but sometimes as effective. The influence of Queen Caroline on George ii of England was considerable, and often when Walpole was in difficulties it was the queen who smoothed his path. This quite reasonable and constructive interference must have been very widely used where the prince and princess got on well.

Less successful perhaps were the attempts by Marie Antoinette to take an active part in politics. In the early stages she had some success, for which she was roundly sat on by her pompous brother. Later he tried to use her himself, but by that time, as she then admitted, she had but little political influence. Of the first attempts Joseph wrote

You meddle in a great many matters which first of all do not concern you, which you know nothing about and in regard to which the cabals and associates who flatter you and know how to arouse your amour propre or desire to shine ... cause you to take one step after another ... certain to bring extreme unpleasantness upon you sooner or later ...

Why do you think it your business, my dear sister, to transfer ministers, to send one to his estates, to have a particular office given to this man or that ... to create a new and expensive post at your court and finally, to talk about public affairs ...?

Have you ever asked yourself by what right you interfere in the affairs of government and the French king? What studies have you ever made ... that you dare to imagine that your advice or opinion can be of any use ...?

Above Maria Theresa may have been a down-to-earth character, but it was nonetheless thought that a bouquet – made in precious stones by J. M. Grossee – would not be out of place or unappreciated. It still exists in the Treasury at Vienna.

Opposite The passion for chinoiserie was by no means limited to outside houses. Wood, plaster, paint or even, as here at the Spanish palace of Aranjuez, Buenretiro porcelain might serve to panel rooms with all the fantasy of this delicious style. This room was finished in 1765.

If the queen's role was secondary in the pageant of court life, and but a reflection of the honour the sovereign had chosen to bestow upon her, it was at least second lead. At all public functions that were not directly political or military – and even sometimes if they were – the queen was expected to attend, and to appear in a manner of dress and jewels that befitted the wealth and rank of her husband. Though perhaps not the youngest nor the prettiest of the company assembled, the queen was expected to outshine everybody by her manner, bearing and accoutrements. The preparations took hours and often meant getting up at five or six in the morning, when a formal court was to be held, and being subjected to hours of hairdressing, preparation and robing by her ladies-in-waiting, followed by the tedium and monotony of formal presentations and appearances until the time to go home and change again for whatever entertainment the evening might have to offer. If she was unwell these attendances could be really trying, but never for a moment was Majesty allowed to let up. The queens could sit down – often they were the only people who could – but the narratives of ladies-in-waiting suggest that really well trained Highnesses were indestructible. Naturally, to wear the finest clothes and jewels, and to be complimented on every side as the first lady of the land, had its attractions, but one may well suspect that many agreed with Miss Burney's 'sweet Queen', that after the first flush of excitement this pleasure soon wore off and could become a bore, though one to be endured for its duty and rewards.

Any deviation from form and etiquette was not expected even in queens, and could bring sharp rebuke and a reminder that the queen was there as consort and expected to behave as such. There is the story of the Queen of Prussia who was inordinately fond of snuff: on the occasion of the coronation it is related that 'she watched for a long time for an opportunity and when she thought His Majesty did not observe her, she stole out her snuff box'. Unfortunately His Majesty did observe and, without hesitation, sent across a lord-in-waiting to enquire 'whether she remembered the place where she was and the rank she held there'. This story is very indicative of the whole attitude of royal life and the queen's position in it.

Eternal dressing up in full state, always with the same attendants, interminable formal drawing rooms and apartments with little else to do but exchange platitudes and gossip, operas, concerts, reading and the same few faces day after day, must quickly have proved sterile to anyone with any sparkle of intelligence. Hunting, for those who pursued it, was a relief, as was gambling. These activities apart, there was little else besides the bedding, pregnancies, birth and yet more bedding of which Maria Leczynska complained so bitterly – or neglect. Such a life was of course com-

The movement towards wilting femininity in queens was not really completed until the sentimentality of 19th-century thought had taken control of the whole continent of Europe. This trend could scarcely be better represented than in this double portrait of Queen Maria Theresa and Queen Adelaide at Turin.

mon to all upper-class women, for whom work – other than good works – was not allowed, but at least these women could choose those to whom they wished to speak and carry on a reasonable and open conversation. Rarely was this permitted to queens. Nor was the chatting up of queens encouraged. As Queen Charlotte complained to Fanny Burney, it was heavy, when all the time one had to initiate the conversation, since etiquette forbade anyone to start a subject before royalty, and even then, as the person addressed was usually so scared that she could only mutter back in monosyllables, there was but little interchange.

Ambassadors

In a world where all political action was conducted as an inter-family affair with each royalty trying to get the best bargain from the cousinage, ambassadors were important. Since every decision in almost every land ultimately rested on one man, the nature of any outside representative was manifestly a first consideration. As court gossip rather than the word of princes or ministers was likely to give the key to the real state of affairs, the need to be agreeable and gregarious was essential. Since everyone was likely to bring divergent opinions and comments – often deliberately planted – a capacity for astute personal assessment was highly desirable. Equally, a facility to lie superbly, bluff, dissimulate and still be the life and soul of the party was necessary. Since Foreign Offices virtually did not exist and distances between one capital and another were considerable, with no quicker contact than the horse, an ambassador really could act – and was expected to – without having a train of changing foreign secretaries breathing down his neck. All this required an extremely capable, if not necessarily a brilliant man. To be acceptable in eighteenth-century terms he also had to be a gentleman and, in normal circumstances, the higher rank the better. As Queen Anne rather clumsily expressed herself 'I doubt his birth will not entitle him to be envoy'. 'Him' was the writer Matthew Prior, who had been successfully carrying on negotiations for a Treaty with France in 1712.

Prior had been appointed by the then curiously liberal and democratic government which believed in using its writers and intellectuals. He had been the go-between and the responsible agent in this rather shady and questionable deal. As the packhorse for a government he was good enough, but as the personal representative of a crowned head at a final treaty – which was, in fact, a personal agreement between two sovereigns – he would not do. The point that should be emphasized is that Queen Anne was perfectly right, in the perspective of the day. She had nothing against Prior intellectually, or he would not have been appointed in the first place, but a monarch's representative for great occasions had to be an aristocrat. He might be far stupider, as was the duke she first appointed to take over this negotiation, who fortunately managed to be killed in a duel before leaving for France. A

The portrait of an ambassador: Sir William Hamilton, envoy to the Neapolitan court, painted in Italy in 1775 by David Allen. Though more well-known in history as the husband of Nelson's Emma, Sir William was, in fact, a very useful and serious ambassador. His great passion for collecting did not immediately profit his king as Nicodemus Tessin's did the King of Sweden, but later the British Museum inherited many items from his collection.

monarch who would not receive leading intellectuals among his own subjects, on the grounds that they were middle-class, was unlikely to be put into the best negotiating humour if a commoner was presented to him as his cousin's representative. Indeed, such an insult could have wrecked a treaty, and prevented the cessation of a ruinous war which the nations as a whole were profoundly thankful to see finished. The previous treaty between Louis and William III had been conducted by one of the most splendid envoys, the new Earl of Portland. The fact that Portland had only very recently been ennobled for services as open favourite of the king did not matter at all. Royal command had made him an earl and earls were respectable – socially at least. Besides, his training was superb.

In addition to all the social activities, which still prevail in some degree today, the accredited representatives of the monarch had many other duties to perform. As marriage brokers between royal families they often had a busy time. More clandestine perhaps were the occasions when they were called upon to weigh and assess the desirability of some princess or prince for this purpose. This was not unreasonable, since such alliances were usually the consummation of some wider political activity upon which the ambassador had been long engaged. Then, again, ambassadors were naturally in a position to make nice exotic purchases, especially wines and works of art. They were also, and more significantly, heads of an elaborate observation and espionage network. In the absence of any contemporary media except rather scrappy newspapers, it was difficult, almost impossible, to know the general climate of opinion whether among 'cousin' kings or their ministers. The only thing of which anyone could be certain was that few of them told the truth, or at least not the whole truth. It was therefore very necessary to have other means of getting information. Discretion was an occupational necessity for monarchs, but with it came a delight in espionage that almost ranked with architecture and hunting. No holds were barred, from murder to censorship. Private correspondence was a particularly fruitful source of information both on foreign affairs and on disaffected subjects, and it was useful for blackmail. Codes were extensively used, as was every practice of cross and double cross in planted or substituted correspondence. Bribery, cheating and lies were the daily fare, and every ambassador was expected to be an adept at how much, when and where to do any of these things. Royal mistresses and ministers were special game; everyone knew every move since they all played themselves. It added spice to a rather unvaried life.

A good example of the complicated situations that might be created is offered by the agreeable story of how Count Seckendorf was planted as Austrian envoy on the irascible and difficult

Above It did not do for an ambassador to live in a way that was anything less than princely. Even if most were already rich, few expected to do something for nothing. One of the customary English perquisites was to give the ambassador elect a grant upon the Treasury for 'plate'. One of the elaborate services created in this way included these tureens by Kändler and candelabra by Le Sage. Sometimes the services had to be returned, but obviously most people tried to keep them.

Right The arrogance of expression exemplified in this letter – even if by 1852 it had become mere ritual – shows exactly the way a baroque royal thought. It was *my* subject, *my* confidence, *my* country, and *my* decision whether I would go to war against *my* enemies.

Frederick William of Prussia. The count had fought in battle with the king and was a great charmer. It was arranged that he should walk on the esplanade before the palace at the regular hour when the king came to smoke his pipe at the window. The old comrade-in-arms was observed and bidden to come in. Majesty insisted that his stay should be prolonged beyond the two days ostensibly planned en route to Scandinavia. The count could not but comply. He stayed – for years – as had been designed. After a few months he had bribed anyone of use and his value to the Austrian court was formidable. The whole business had, in any case, been planned by the venal first minister – against payment, of course. There are many such stories, which well illustrate autocratic politics and power.

Slightly more elaborate, perhaps, were the ways of Sir Charles Hanbury-Williams, English ambassador to the court of Augustus II of Poland and Saxony, and later to that of St Petersburg. Reduced to essentials, the story was that during his term of office in Dresden he had met and favoured a very charming and handsome young Polish nobleman, Stanislas Poniatowski. The boy joined his

Osborne House, 4th December, 1852.

SIR, MY BROTHER,
Being desirous to maintain uninterrupted the union and good understanding which happily subsist between Great Britain and France, I have made choice of Lord Cowley, a peer of my United Kingdom, a member of my Privy Council, and Knight Commander of the Most Honourable Order of the Bath, to reside at your Imperial Majesty's Court in the character of my Ambassador Extraordinary and Plenipotentiary. The long experience which I have had of his talents and zeal for my service assures me that the choice which I have made of Lord Cowley will be perfectly agreeable to your Imperial Majesty, and that he will prove himself worthy of this new mark of my confidence. I request that your Imperial Majesty will give entire credence to all that Lord Cowley shall communicate to you on my part, more especially when he shall assure your Imperial Majesty of my invariable attachment and esteem, and shall express to you those sentiments of sincere friendship and regard with which I am, Sir, my Brother, your Imperial Majesty's good Sister,
VICTORIA R.
To my good Brother, the Emperor of the French."

121

staff and in 1756 when the ambassador moved to Russia, Ponia-towski moved too. Shortly, through the good offices of Sir Charles, Poniatowski was appointed representative of his own monarch, Augustus of Saxony. Both wanted a finger in the Russian pie. The upshot of this diplomatic combination was that Sir Charles be-came a father figure and confidant to the Grand Duchess Ekaterina Alexievna, young wife of the heir apparent and later, Catherine the Great. By this means he could flatter, bribe or advise the prin-cess for British ends. Poniatowski on the other hand became her lover at Sir Charles' introduction – which of course made another friend at court. A liaison of this kind was very unusual, but the situation was facilitated by the husband, who had other interests. This fairy-story had a very happy ending, as a few years later, the Empress Catherine – as she had by then become – was able through her influence to ensure Stanislas' election as King of Poland.

Poniatowski must indeed have had a way with him as, even earlier, he entirely captivated the aged Paris blue-stocking Mme Geoffrin with whom he struck up an intimate mother-son rela-tionship in the most romantic eighteenth-century manner. When he acceded to the throne, Mme Geoffrin visited Warsaw to see him. Catherine then expected the poor old lady to travel on to St Pe-tersburg, and when she failed their relationship and long cor-respondence was quickly stopped.

As an insight into an ambassador's function in dynastic mar-riage negotiations no better illustration is offered than by all the absurdities concerning the betrothal and marriage of Marie An-toinette to Louis XVI. The Empress Maria Theresa had been very anxious for this match in order to bring to an end the hostilities that had grumbled on between France and Austria throughout the century. Louis XV, or rather his minister, Choiseul, was not so con-vinced. Their ambassador at Vienna, M. de Durfort, was directly instructed to play hot and cold and not to commit himself. The task was not always easy, as the empress used to take public oc-casions to try and involve him. Finally, in 1769, the betrothal was arranged. Then the trouble really began, and all of it concerned the endless minutiae of protocol and etiquette, rather than the serious politics which had lain at the root of the match, or any consideration for the feelings of either of the two children in-volved. 'The wording of the marriage contract, the form of public entry, the process or the solemn demand, the formalities for es-corting the bride, even the ceremonial to be observed towards the Ambassador Extraordinary in all the functions he would have to carry out'. This last was vitally important. Durfort was specifically instructed no longer to invite the princess to the embassy for, 'the respect that M. de Durfort, as a subject of the king, will from that moment [the formal betrothal] owe the princess will no longer

Opposite Although he might get plate and pay from home, it would have been a sorry case if an ambassador did not receive some costly recognition from the poten-tate to whom he was assigned. Most, unless very displeasing, were rewarded in cash or kind, more or less according to the goodwill or the services that might be rendered. This gold snuff box was in fact made for the hunting suit of Augustus the Strong, but is typical of the sort of present such a prince would give to an acceptable ambassador. Others would receive services of porcelain or plate.

Overleaf It is ironical that one of the most magnificent ambassadorial receptions known to us from history should have been accorded to some extremely questionable envoys (see p. 143). Coming at the end of his reign and life, it was almost a swan-song of magnificent display for Louis XIV and was so regarded even at the time. The reception was far more for the passing Sun King than for the Persian ambassadors. The painting is attributed to F. Coypel.

permit him to seek or invite this honour'. Perhaps the height of the farce was reached when, on Easter Sunday, M. de Durfort left Vienna as Ambassador in *Ordinary* to turn round in the road and return an hour later with an enormous train of forty-eight carriages, as Ambassador *Extraordinary* with a suite of a hundred or more persons in gorgeous new livery. The empress and Joseph II formally received their old friend the next day, with similar pomp and etiquettes. So the play of balls and dinners began. The final party at which nine royals, eating off gold plate, were watched by some hundred and fifty nobles was not attended by Durfort, as etiquette would have made him give precedence to a lesser German princeling related to the family. As representative of the king of France and future father-in-law, this was undesirable. It was therefore agreed that he should stay at home.

In this case the precedence issue possibly had some justification, but very often the quarrels and sulks and insults that flew about over ambassadorial claims to precedence were an unending source of trouble. James I had instituted a chef de protocol to set aright the quarrels of his foreign representatives; William III had had to use all his royal power to stop a duel. The stories are unending and arose sometimes from zeal on the royal master's behalf and honour and, more often one suspects, on purely personal grounds, where His Excellency had become more royal than the royals. The kind of ludicrous situation which could arise is illustrated by the story of the two ambassadors of France and Spain whose coaches met head on in a narrow street in the Hague. Both refused to budge, and their attendants were about to fight it out when members of the Dutch Assembly came up and at least prevented bloodshed. It then took the leading Dutch members four hours and nightfall to get agreement, which was only obtained by cutting through the paling at the side of the road and thus giving access to a dual carriageway that ran the other side. The Spanish ambassador was given a priority for this new track as compensation for giving way. The general consensus of opinion in this matter was that the Frenchman had won. Indeed, so tiresome could these people become that England's George II begged his cousins to send ordinary envoys to save all the trouble, expense and formality which he hated in equal shares.

Quite apart from its demonstration of consummate luxury and extravagance, this figure in silver gilt, jewels and enamels was made by the Dinglinger workshop early in the 18th century for the Saxon court, to hold a collection of emeralds which had been presented to an earlier Elector in 1581 by Emperor Rudolph II. When not engaged purely in politics or espionage, it was ambassadors who bore such special gifts from one royal highness to another, usually to pave the way for friendlier thinking on some point at issue, to prepare for a treaty or to gain an ally.

Mistresses

Perhaps the greatest paradox of all is that of the royal mistresses, by whom we mean not so much casuals who may have indulged the royal pleasure, but the accepted 'maîtresses en titre', whose whoredom won them titles, honours and wealth, and many of whom played an important part in the conduct of their nations. Monarchs had always had mistresses and many are famous in history, but the attachments of baroque princes were perhaps more flauntingly displayed than usual.

As a recent historian pithily noted 'the practice of monarchy combines the maximum of temptation with the maximum of opportunity'. Nevertheless, this did not make the acceptance of mistresses always very easy. The pious were genuinely shocked and feared for their king's hereafter; others, from jealousy or pique, were ready to attack whenever possible. The grounds were generally moral and it must be admitted that what these mistresses gave the monarch would have earned them a whipping, penance or imprisonment in the outside world. At the same time, considering the general level of behaviour among the upper classes, it was stretching hypocrisy a very long way to condemn a mistress for whom most women would willingly have stood in (or, perhaps, in this case, lain down) at any time.

When the lady was not of noble birth, the snobbery of class was also brought into the attack. Here, perhaps, the grounds were more genuine. There was something inimical to the foundation of all order if Highness should demean itself too far – especially if other persons of quality were called upon to meet the lady and be civil. Some baroque monarchs countered the class issue by making their established ladies duchesses, which automatically gave them precedence over all but the royal family and a few of the very highest in the land. It must have given more than one ruler wry amusement to see some particularly self-righteous and bitter critic of his love compelled to humble herself and give precedence every time his mistress passed.

Apart from the question of maximum temptations and maximum opportunity, the existence of these mistresses must have arisen almost inevitably from the circumstances of royal life. For a man to be married as a teenager to someone he might never have

A drawing by J. H. Fragonard, now in the museum at Besançon.

seen and who perhaps did not even speak his language, was not necessarily the best foundation for lasting happiness. Duty done, enthusiasm might wane and someone more in accord with natural taste find favour. The sheer formalities demanded by etiquette must also have been inhibiting. It cannot have been conducive to friendly intimacy if one had to call a husband or wife 'Your Majesty' all the time, often in private as well as public. Furthermore, position, as well as all the spying, intrigue, hypocrisy and flattery of court, made friendship, as the outside world might know it, difficult. Little wonder that these spoiled but generally human animals fell in love – for often it was just as simple as that. As d'Argenson wrote of Louis xv 'the king is more independent now he has a mistress; it is astonishing how it matures a prince to have a mistress'.

This cynical eighteenth-century comment is indicative of the truth and if, upon occasion, we can read wife for mistress, in most cases the word meant what it said. Great mistresses like Mme de Pompadour held their lovers as much by their minds and companionship as by their bodies, though the mind did not always need to be of a very high standard. Jolly and less educated girls like Nell Gwyn or O'Murphy served their purpose through the uncomplicated nature of the liaison, and the difference needs to be appreciated. Bishop Burnet records of Charles ii and the Duchess of Cleveland that 'his passion for her and her strange behaviour to him did so disorder him that often he was not master of himself, nor capable of minding business'. This statement comes from the writer who could say of the same monarch that 'he had a very ill opinion of both men and women' and that 'he thought that nobody did serve him out of love and so he was quits with all the world, and loved others as little as he thought they loved him'. Time and again we read in letters and diaries how other princes seem to have been similarly affected by wayward womenfolk they took 'en titre'. Even so redoubtable a character as Catherine the Great could be disturbed (though not much more) if she thought one of her serious lovers had been unkind.

Given the circumstances of absolutism, it is manifest that any mistress who could hold an absolute monarch in thrall was likely to be in a position of considerable power. She was indeed. Some, like their own lovers, used the chances well and others ill, according to their natures. Some used them for purely personal ends, acquiring wealth, land and titles for themselves and their families. These, generally, tended to overplay their hand and were replaced, with or without loss of gains. Others liked to meddle in politics, which was not only interesting, but added further to their power from the support of grateful ministers and courtiers. In any event it was an accepted practice of the time that any appointments

Charles ii of England by Honoré Pelle. The more prurient, or envious of later generations have speculated as to which royal was 'the greatest whoremaster of them all'. Since princes were concerned with their own pleasure and found no need to enter any wider competition, they did not keep game books for researchers. Folklore makes its attributions and Charles would seem to be in the running.

These pretty things; very much
how their masters no doubt saw
them. Clodion's happy satyrs
(above) are carefree. Domenico
Mondo drew an ideal fantasy *(left)*.
The O'Murphy *(top right)*,
Louis xv's girl mistress, was
painted many times by Boucher.
Clodion again *(right)* indulged
fantasy in terracotta, as did
another artist *(far right)* with more
modesty.

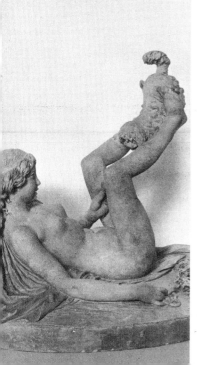

or favours that the mistress might be able to obtain from the king were to be paid for. The princes knew this perfectly well and aided and abetted their mistresses in the continuance of so sensible a tradition, which kept everyone happy and also helped to pay expenses. Some ladies had a perfectly well known fee, at least for regular requests – so much for a title, so much for a cornetcy, so much for a regiment, and so on. Cash not competence was what counted, though even a very stupid mistress was unwilling to prejudice her own case by an approach which would obviously be unpopular.

It would be unrealistic to imagine that anyone became a prince's 'maîtresse en titre' by accident or just out of love, or fun, though all these elements may have played some part. No one who did not want the job could have put up with the social and moral difficulties, the jealousies and opposition that were always welling up under the surface, however successful the incumbent might be. Nor would they have put up with the nervous strains that the life imposed. Insecurity of tenure is always any mistress's hazard but with these royal attachments the more so, as the lover was likely to be even more spoilt and whimsical than ordinary men. Then too, the competition was greater and the opposition plots unending. Furthermore, loss of the job might mean loss for friends and family as well. It could even mean loss of liberty or life, though on the whole, apart from banishment, most monarchs seem to have behaved reasonably well to those who had been with them.

By the very nature of their existence baroque princes were selfish, and seldom willing to adjust their whims to other people's needs or wishes. Few liked disease or kept a mistress who became sick or tiresome. Louis xiv's women suffered tortures through his utter lack of consideration when they were having a period, a pregnancy, or even bladder trouble on the interminable long journeys in coaches over shocking roads. The king never stopped for anyone's needs but his own, and to have insisted otherwise would have been unwise indeed. On one occasion when Louis xv was ill, Mme de Pompadour had hysterics of fear that he might suddenly become religious and repentant, as he had once done, and so dismiss her. Naturally, her enemies rejoiced. On such occasions court gossip and speculation rose to fever heat. This time one hostile lady came to the marquise and informed her that the king had given instructions that she was to pack her bags and go. Torn with distraction, she packed and was only prevented from leaving by a more friendly member of the court who advised her to stay until more formal orders came. The king recovered and the liaison continued happily until her death. Apart from such potentially major threats, a host of minor pinpricks were just a part of the life. Baroque courtiers, especially royals, were adept at discomforting

Hardly anything could be more significant of eighteenth-century exoticism and extravagance than this chamber-pot made by the Dresden porcelain factory and decorated by the *hausmaler* Heroldt.

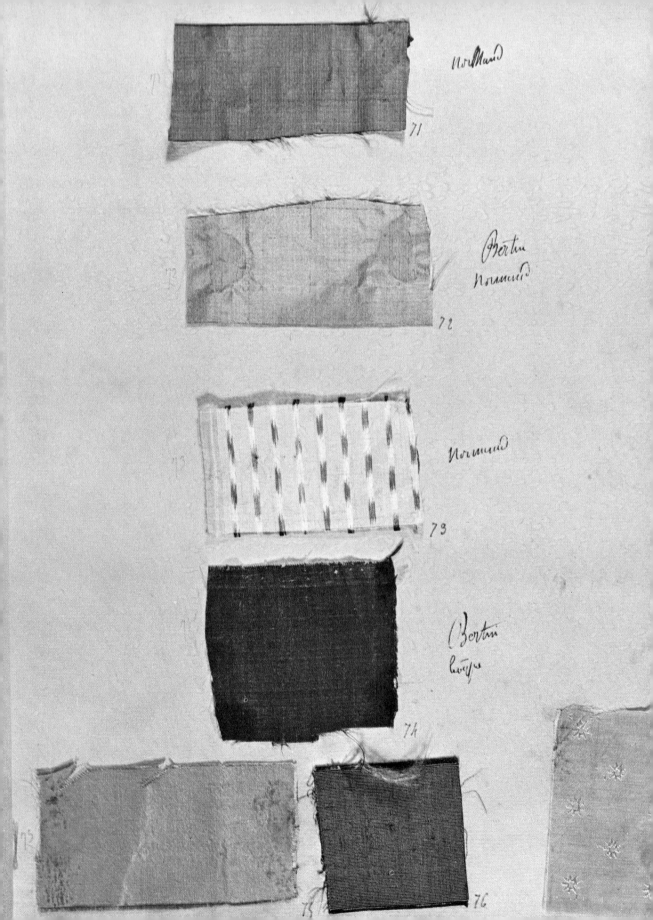

Wethland

71

Bertin
Normand

72

Normand

73

Bertin
loupe

74

75

76

those they did not like and often childishly delighted to exercize their talent. For instance, the king used to set Mme de Pompadour in a carriage with the royal ladies of the court, a bizarre piece of mischief, knowing how they all disliked each other. The royals riposted by refusing to speak to her, since they could not refuse to go, even if they had wanted to. Such little discomforts were continuous and carefully planned by opponents, who acted like children ganging up on an unpopular member of the school. Lampoons, quips in plays, innuendoes in the press or even physical attacks on the coach were regular fare. Occasionally revenge was sweet, as when one courtier was so foolish as to be traced as the author of a leaflet of scurrilous rhymes. He was sent to prison for twenty years.

The mistress could also be a subtle way of attacking the prince, by accusing her of leading Majesty astray and even of witchcraft, in which all believed and many dabbled.

If witchcraft and philtres were sparingly used for this purpose, the antics in which women of the eighteenth century indulged to try and mitigate the ravages of time were legion. Not only was the life span shorter, but the prevalence of disease and the sorry state of medicine menaced life, looks and figures. Smallpox, wasting or fattening ailments, poor teeth and worse dentists threatened everyone, but were disastrous for a mistress, for whom a pocked face, a lost figure or halitosis might not be just misfortunes but – as the beautiful Aurora von Königsmarck found out – the end. Above all the fear of venereal disease must have been present, though possibly not so much with a royal lover as with those more ambulant of less degree. The little note 'You will leave for your property at X ... and not present yourself at Court again' might be dictated for many reasons, but none, perhaps, so frequent as decline of interest in a fading beauty.

Some women could arrange to substitute their mind and company for sex and even encouraged their lovers to go outside for the latter, though this was manifestly risky. Others, like the mistresses who delighted George I of England and Hanover, had less to worry about, since he did not mind them old and fat or scraggy. In fact he had one of each for many years. The rakish Regent d'Orléans was one of many credited with the pithy but questionable comment that 'all cats are grey in the dark'.

Many found honourable retirement and it is a curious feature of the phenomenon of princes that succeeding incumbents generally respected their forbears' alliances. Just as well, perhaps, for some, as there would be many a dukedom less if they had not been so accommodating. 'God, who'd have thought we three whores should have met here' was a spirited comment from one ennobled ex-Stuart mistress to two other relics of succeeding monarchs as they

Mistresses, queens and all the court devoted enormous care to their clothes. For the privileged, as for the trade, then and now, the weavers produced cards with samples of materials, although these particular fabrics were from dresses already made up in the wardrobe of Marie Antoinette. Each day the patterns would be brought by her Mistress of the Wardrobe and the Queen would decide what to wear. This card dates from 1789.

The rewards of royals' whores and gigolos could be magnificent and go far beyond estates and titles. In 1771 Catherine the Great ordered this terrine *(above)* as part of a service for her lover Orloff from the Paris silversmith J. N. Roettiers. In the same year Mme du Barry commissioned the Sèvres porcelain *(far right)* which carries her initials. More exquisite still is the gold mounted ewer and basin *(right)* which the Pompadour once owned and which Queen Marie Antoinette was happy to inherit.

were all being entertained at the newly established Hanoverian court.

The stakes were high, and the game risky, but the winnings for those who were successful could be enormous: power, position and wealth beyond dreams. If we refer yet again to Mme de Pompadour it is because she is the archetype, and also so attractive, but dozens of others acted similarly if less elegantly. Mme de Pompadour having ensnared the king – and this was quite deliberate and took some time – played her cards superbly. Though of bourgeois origin, her family had been of reasonable circumstances, if, sometimes, of questionable morality. Her husband was a gentleman and she had many literary and intellectual contacts. This background, after a period of training in court etiquettes, enabled her to be brought into Versailles. Tactful, charming, gracious, lovely and intelligent, her rise was swift. Unlike some of her profession, she was at pains to speak well of everybody and to make every deference to the queen, and thus she avoided creating more enemies than was inevitable in her position. Soon she was marquise with estates of her own. She got titles and position for her brother, now created Marigny, whose competence and ability did much for French arts, as did his sister's patronage. Then began sterner tests of power. The leading minister had seen fit to be her enemy, and she held him responsible for many lampoons and jests about her. Maurepas received a royal order to leave for his estates near Bourges within forty-eight hours, not to return and not to leave them. He languished there for twenty-five years until recalled by Louis XVI.

The mistress had won, and such a victory could not but raise her stock. The young Comte de Cheverny, in charge of ambassadorial affairs, recalled that all representatives except the papal nuncio called on the favourite after making their formal presentations to

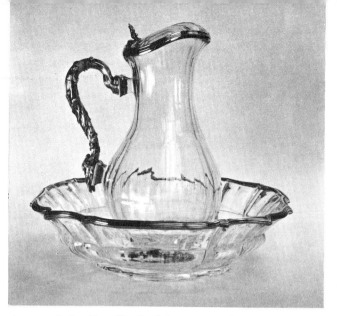

the royal family. She had begun to play a part in international affairs.

Perhaps her most remarkable achievements were when she had ceased to live physically with the king but nonetheless managed to retain her power and position as friend and adviser. Fortunately for her, he had by then extended his taste to teenagers and kept some in little houses of their own with staffs and teachers, the establishment known as the Parc aux Cerfs. It was peopled by the king's valet and visited 'incognito', by which piece of double thinking Majesty's philanderings among the proletariat could be glossed over. While he took his pleasure with these saucy kittens, Mme de Pompadour reigned supreme over his mind – such as it was. An interesting sidelight on the whole paradoxical situation arises from the fact that once she had ceased to be his mistress it was felt respectable to keep her at court as one of the dames du palais in attendance on the queen. Reasonably enough in the circumstances, many thought it rather quixotic that this honour should be conferred upon her by her ex-lover, but this is not so surprising to us, perhaps, as the fact that she then formally wrote to her husband – for she was still married to M. le Normant d'Etiolles – to ask if she might accept.

To add further to the strangeness of eighteenth-century thinking, in her new capacity she attended the queen to mass every day. Though penitence does not seem to have gone very far with her as it did with some other exalted Magdalens, she had had a convent training, and the insurance policy element may have been somewhere in the back of the mind even of this friend of atheists and encyclopaedists. The king himself conveniently overcame any superstitions there might be by telling himself and others that as God's delegate on earth he would not be allowed to suffer in the hereafter, adding, for further comfort, that he would have ex-

By this time Mme de Pompadour's power and influence was enormous, Ministers, warned by the fate of Maurepas and further successful banishments, took heed. Perhaps her greatest political coup was the treaty with Austria achieved directly through her intervention. For this the Empress Maria Theresa herself did not hesitate to make acknowledgment with accompanying largesse of a portrait in a diamond frame. The favourite's reply in thanks was, of course, approved both by the king and his minister. Such could be the rewards of successful waiting on an absolute monarch.

As we know from the case of Catherine the Great, the sex roles could easily be reversed. Apart from passing fancies, her great lovers, like Orloff or Potemkin, achieved equal success, gaining titles, wealth and honours and taking even greater part in national affairs. For monarchs with homosexual tastes the stories are identical; the same risks, the same gains, for those who were obliging.

It is one of the interesting aspects of the situation that the resulting bastards were not very often recognized – at least in the eighteenth century. As we have seen, the seventeenth century was still fairly robust about these matters and Louis XIV made no bones about the Duke du Maine and others while Charles II also gave his luckier ones dukedoms. In general, however, these persons were spirited away. Complaisant husbands might give name and shelter at a price, and obvious outlets, such as convents, were exploited but, on the whole, by the eighteenth century some decent reticence was held desirable. Louis XV was explicit and careful that the results of his activities in the Parc aux Cerfs should be given to 'poor' foster parents or servants, and if provision was made the matter was discreetly handled, which avoided embarrassment and importunity. Besides, an extensive proletarian strain – with royal bar sinister – was undesirable.

The most spectacular whoremaster, even including Charles II of England and the Regent d'Orléans, was probably Augustus of Saxony. He is accredited by his Prussian cousin, Princess Wilhelmina, with well over three hundred illegitimate offspring. Exact or not, this maidenly tribute appears admiring rather than critical and is yet another indication of the apartness of a prince.

When the mistress lost out the situation was often sad. Even if still left with possessions, she was generally ostracized as being of no further significance or influence. There is the pathetic story of one who jostled some ordinary worshippers in church when making her way to pray at the altar. 'Fine carry on for a tart' said a bystander, who might well have been whipped for such temerity when the lady was in power. The ex-mistress turned and said sadly, 'as you recognize me, why not pray for my soul?'

Opposite Since Christ had accepted the outcast Magdalen, she became accepted by the Church and thus offered consolation and hope to those who had erred and to more who wanted to. Representations were numerous – always in penitence. The terracotta *(above)* is again by Clodion; the ivory *(below)* emphasizes the wider spread of the cult, being by an unknown artist of less quality.

Below A porcelain figure of Augustus of Saxony, who earned – and apparently richly deserved – his nickname of 'the Strong' on this battlefield.

Exotica

One of the more curious reflections of the mystique of royalty and one that reveals the attitudes underlying the baroque mind is to be found in the treatment of exotic royals – or at least those embassies which came from distant parts. Most people in the seventeenth and eighteenth centuries were entirely fascinated by the thought of oriental potentates and tended to invest them with a power so absolute that it made the western monarchs quite conformist. There is no reason to think that princes did not feel the same. Contemporary stories about the east abound with utter fantasy. Even the most absolute of baroque princes could not think in terms of the Arabian Nights or go so far as to tie a teasing mistress in a bag and throw her in the Bosphorus. But this did not mean that they might not very much have liked to; and stories of this kind must have presented happy dreams for those inhibited by Christian teaching. Then there were the tales of the magnificence in gold and slaves and jewellery, and wealth which even national heads could not amass in Europe. There was also a certain fairytale attraction bound up with this unknown world where djinns and magic were part and parcel of the lacquer and porcelain and ormolu which stood upon the mantlepiece. This was the world that Dinglinger created in his gold and jewels for Augustus of Saxony. All this had become part of that theatrical projection which made their lives enjoyable, especially when the facts were too far off to counter or deny.

It is a thousand pities that no great eastern potentate paid a visit to a wealthy European court. The show would have been fantastic. As it was, even before the envoys of these 'cousins' of such splendour and magnificence, most western monarchs put on quite an effort, though there could be something of a backwash about heathens, infidels and such. Even if it was quite reasonable to send out ships to plunder 'blackamoors' and sell them off for slaves, as the Muslim pirates did to any western seamen that they found, the state of 'cousinage' insisted that royals anywhere, and of whatever shade, should be accorded all the honours due.

This Western attitude was paramount in Louis XIV's last magnificent reception for a very dubious Persian envoy. So great was the mystery of the Orient that even this almighty monarch felt

This clock is packed with eighteenth-century ideas on exotic persons. Mounted in Paris, the porcelain figures are Chinese representations of a kind of Afro-Asian creature. European chinoiserie presents an equally fantastic idea of a Chinaman, and there is no doubt that in a way western princes so thought of their oriental counterparts and vice versa.

There are rather sinister political overtones to this figure carved in India and presented by the French to Tipu Sahib, a potentate with curious delights. The tiger is portrayed consuming an English Company man, and its stomach contains organ machinery designed to enhance the verisimilitude by adding groans and cries.

constrained to put on a show that few contemporary royals would have rated. It was like playing at really grown up fairy-tales, and it too. Pöllnitz, who was an eye witness, has left a description of the scene.

The King's Throne, which was at one end, and raised very high, was of a Gold Ground, with Flowers and The Arms of France embroidered on it. The King was dressed in a Suit of Coffee-colour'd Velvet, adorn'd with Jewels to the value of several Millions. The young Dauphin was at his Majesty's Right Hand in a robe of Gold Brocade, adorn'd with Diamonds and Pearls. The Duke of Orleans was on his left, dressed in a Suit of Blue Velvet, adorn'd with a gold Spanish Point, seeded with very beautiful Diamonds and Pearls. The Princes of the Blood, the legitimated Princes, the Prince of Dombes and the Count d'Eu, both sons to the Duke of Maine sat in the same row, on the right and left of the King.

The writer then goes on to detail the vast assembly of richly dressed nobles of the highest rank who stood in tiers on either side, as well as the regiments in full dress lining the staircases and galleries, though it was noted that 'The Splendour of the Soldiery was very much lessened by a Great Quantity of Rain'.

No whit more justified, perhaps, but much more sympathetic was all the fuss accorded in the 1770s to 'Prince' Omai, a pretty boy brought back by Captain Cook from Otaheiti. Allegedly a chieftain's son, the princely title was accorded and he visited the king and queen. London society lionized him and Sir Joshua Reynolds was most happy to paint his portrait – and a lovely thing it is. Justified by the 'royal' association, the popular imagination had imbued this charming youth with qualities which set him quite apart from other Negro boys or Indians that eighteenth-century society kept as pets – when they did not make them slaves. He was credited with the possession of the something 'extra' that set him on a par with other royalties – or nearly so. The mystery had worked again.

The same reflection of exotic attitudes is found in Charles I of England's herald painter who was also paid to send illuminated letters to 'The Emperor and Petrach of Russia, The Grand Signior, The Great Mogul, The Emperor of Persia and the Kings of Bantam, Macassar, Barbary, Fez . . . and other far distant Kings'. In the eighteenth century Sir Thomas Brand was 'Embellisher of Letters to the Eastern Princes'.

Another facet of the interest in these exotica is to be found in a narrative of the *History of Europe for 1765,* published in Venice in 1783. While carefully recording important events such as war and peace, this small volume finds it purposeful to tell the world that when visiting King George III of England his excellency 'Haman Aga Josa Effendi', ambassador of His Majesty the King of Tripoly had brought as presents 'A collection of Ancient Arabic Manuscripts, with 12 fine Horses, 6 Lions, 2 Tigers, 4 Ostriches, an Eagle and a magnificently decorated Saddle'. Such a tastefully balanced contribution to the library, stables and menageries suggests that His Tripolitanian Majesty, or his advisers, must have been agreeably civilized.

The sanctity of royal position, and the regard given to princes as beings apart was not limited to Europe. When, for instance, King Charles XII of Sweden found himself in Turkish hands, cut off by his defeat at Poltava, the sultan courteously befriended him, providing hospitality and a pension over the years, because he was a king, albeit a defeated one. His thanks from Charles were more in keeping with what stories looked for in a Paynim heathen than a Christian knight, but despite very questionable behaviour, the mystique of Charles's royal apartness held and so this tiresome hero lived to massacre some more. It would be jejune to suppose that the sultan did not think he might conceivably be useful, but primarily, it seems, it was his rank that counted.

The Prince Travels

'Queen Elizabeth slept here' is a notice that was a tourist draw long before the twentieth century and it underlines the practice of royal progress that renaissance princes had inherited from early times. They were part of government, of keeping in touch. In distant areas these visits were the wonder of a decade and people even ruined themselves for the honour of receiving royalty. This could, upon occasion, be policy: it was better that a subject with ideas above his station should pledge his credit over years to make a three day show for royal entertainment than save it up to buy retainers to make trouble. He could be knighted if the effort were sufficient and find the title cheaply bought. Such royal tours persisted at the start of the seventeenth century, but in general, once absolutist monarchs had set themselves apart, most ceased to travel in this way. They tended to keep themselves to themselves and sleep in their own homes, of which they had as many as they wanted anyway. Occasionally they might stay in the house of royal relations.

In smaller states and towns, or in the country, a sovereign prince might condescend to visit in the town, play cards or gamble or receive some hospitality. But in the larger capitals this was not the usual practice. Occasionally the sovereign attended a civic reception or set out on an organized state tour. Then he might descend upon some duke or nobleman who was allowed the honour and expense of such a royal visitation. More generally a house was requisitioned for the royal party.

On official visits, only undertaken for some special reason – to review a fleet, or visit a victorious army in the field – the trains were often most spectacular. The reason was manifestly propagandist. Streets were decorated, tapestries hung out, feasting and wine laid on and formal banquets and receptions, with the inevitable operas, ballets, fun and fireworks added. Not only was the final city to be visited likely to be mulcted, but any towns or villages en route were called upon to make some effort of display. Flowered arches, pealing bells and loyal demonstrations marked the way. This all cost money and sometimes heartbreak if, as might happen, Highness was late or feeling unreceptive and so flashed by without a stop.

This enchanting fantasy from the front of an Austrian or German royal sleigh carries all the sense of occasion as well as of the decoration, beauty and extravagance which accompanied royal travel in the 18th century. Such prettiness may have helped to overcome the practical discomforts of appalling roads and primitive suspension.

Quite apart from the cost of these activities, a real, practical confusion might arise from the sudden addition of hundreds of retainers with their baggage, horses, coaches, waggons and the rest. They all expected to be housed and generally had ideas as to how they should be treated. That a house should be set aside for Majesty was one thing, but for the entourage and valets billets might be modest in extreme. A garret or a passage might be made to serve for sleeping quarters, though by eighteenth-century travel standards these were adequate, if inconvenient for putting on court dress and uniform. Even things like food supplies must have given quite a headache in a world with neither cans nor frigidaires.

From the more personal and intimate point of view the records of those in waiting often give a vivid picture of what they were expected to put up with. Since everyone thought only of the king and queen, the princes and princesses, they may not even have been aware of the needs of court attendants, who were put to strange shifts upon occasion. As Saint Simon noted, 'The most ridiculous incidents do sometimes relieve the most solemn spectacles'. Fanny Burney's description is very telling of how those in attendance on an Oxford visit backed out one by one, covering up for each other as they slipped away to find a friendly waiter with provisions, since their welfare had been forgotten. Sandwiches and apricots were all that could be found and so, clutched in sticky hands, they were munched by starving dignitaries, like children eating chocolate in school. On another occasion a servant had to walk for miles at five o'clock in the morning to find someone capable of doing a court hairdo.

What is surprising in all this is that the arrangements usually went off as well as they did. The detail must have been terrifying and there were no telephones. Everything had to be arranged ahead and schedules made as far as could be without hitch. The slightest breach of protocol and someone, if not Majesty, would be

The finest State coaches employed on great occasions were objects of the most superb magnificence, carved and gilded, the trappings of gold and silver draped with fringe and velvets. This plate (*top*) shows an Austrian State coach as used in the procession illustrated opposite and now in the coach museum at Schönbrunn. Quite a number of these vehicles survive and some, like the English State coach, are still used.

Taken from the series of paintings celebrating the wedding of Joseph II, this shows the elaborate procession for the formal entry of the bride. The cavalcade did not, of course, weave round a vast piazza in this way, but stretched for miles. The painter's convention served to get a full representation onto a manageable canvas.

incensed. Timing, with all the travel hazards of the age, could never be exact.

In addition to the great progresses, there were state occasions when princes visited each other formally. Then every opportunity was taken to show off pomp and circumstance. A splendid example was recorded in June 1660 when the Prince Archbishop of Salzburg paid a formal visit to the Elector of Bavaria. The Archbishop's train was comparatively modest – a mere seven prelates, nine nobles from his household, a confessor, two doctors, six pages, nine trumpeters and an assortment described as '250 head of men and horses'. As he drew near to Munich an advance party of Bavarians came to meet him, consisting of the Crown Prince, the Bishop of

Prints from an engraved souvenir of the State visit of Louis XV to the city of Strasbourg. The elaborate fireworks, the streets hung with tapestries, and not least the lighting with torches of the great spire of the Cathedral represented a prodigious effort of organisation and cost – and fire risk.

Freising, Duke Maximilian and a vast suite of nobles, guards, horses, and carriages. These accompanied the Archbishop to within half an hour of the town of Munich, where the Elector himself came out to welcome them, surrounded by a few regiments of guards in full uniform and the entire court, with state carriages of the first order, guards, populace and servants. As they drew near the two main protagonists descended from their coaches to bid each other welcome. From this point a herald and platoons of burgher guards in Wittelsbach blue and white, with further cohorts of pages, servants and bands, led the procession into the town.

The festivities, which lasted for the best part of a week, included a water festival watched by the Elector and the Archbishop from a specially constructed and heavily decorated barge manoeuvered by one hundred and fifty rowers, and an escorting fleet of lesser

vessels which sailed up the Starnberg See to the accompaniment of waterworks, fireworks, setpieces and displays. On another occasion the slaughter of some four hundred stags accompanied further feasts and fireworks. The setpiece of towers and buildings took three months to construct. Banquets were taken in different halls or palaces each day – all of course especially decorated for the occasion.

Wax candles, thousands upon thousands of them – they were very expensive – together with lanterns lit the palaces and gardens in the evenings. Further decoration was provided by specially planted trees and shrubs, while soldiers in their dress uniforms were used to make up decorative flankings and patterns. Operas and performances in all three theatres which the Elector maintained were taken as a matter of course. The cost was prodigious. The chronicler also added that the nobility all had new clothes every day – fortunately an exceptional case since everything was ultimately paid for either directly or indirectly by the taxed, unfortunate peasantry. The costume climax was provided by the Electress who was arrayed each day in parures of different jewels. ('So many that you could scarcely recognize her!') The famous pearls for the opening, then diamonds, rubies, emeralds and amethysts, in that order, on successive days. She also presented the prizes for such competitions as there were. These were, of course, tactfully awarded to the leaders of the court.

Lesser occasions may not have called forth such exaggeration of display, but prodigious efforts could still be made. This brief description of a visitation by the king and queen of Saxony in the mid-eighteenth century, gives a lively glimpse of what went on.

Their Majesties went into the streets about ten o'clock in a magnificent coach, accompanied by all their courtiers on horseback. Before the Town House they were harangued by the 'Burge-Master' who presented them with a collation in panniers of silver, after which they passed by the house of the Duke of Holstein.

The Front of the House represented The Temple of Glory, the Duke's gentlemen represented the Priests of the Temple, and threw amber and incense into the coals. The Duke's eight children were dressed like Shepherds and Shepherdesses, and brought flowers and recited verses. Several triumphal arches were erected, all the streets were hung with tapestry, and the King set out attended by all the City Companies. His Majesty rode on Horseback, supported by two equerries on foot. His Clothes were of Crimson velvet lined with Ermine and embroidered with Gold, and the buttons were of Diamonds ... His Horse was most richly accoutr'd: The Bit, Stirrups and all the ornaments of the Bridle, were of massy Gold ... The Queen's coach was also of extraordinary magnificence ... When their Majesties were got a quarter of a league out of town, they alighted and got into their Travelling Coaches and received the last compliments from the echevins of the town kneeling bareheaded.

Very colourful, though less vast than the official processions, were the cortèges which accompanied princes on almost any occasion. The book-jacket shows Charles III of Naples on a visit to the Pope, painted by G. P. Pannini. Here we see an arrival at the Quirinal Palace in Rome recorded by Vanvitelli. These pictures are most valuable as showing how the scene must have looked at the time, with all the untidiness, the crowds of beggars, troops, vendors and hangers-on, who filled the piazzas with life. In all this dirt and bustle the royal parties seem to move with absolute detachment, as though they belonged to another world – as indeed was almost true.

To cap the farce, they (Their Majesties) returned into the town by another gate to sleep at the palace, which they left – informally – the next day. This charade was what the people liked and the less formal manner which some monarchs attempted was not appreciated.

Quite apart from the imposition of receptions and the entertainment, the actual travelling must have been a tiring and a boring process. The great lumbering coaches swayed and smelt, the roads (with exception of the very best) were likely to be shocking. To relieve these difficulties princes sometimes went on horseback for much of the way or, on better roads and in decent weather, drove in lighter open carriages. (The danger of attack from highwaymen was not a menace for a royal with his guards.) Sanitary facilities were worse than primitive, unless a stop over at some castle was made. For the immediate royals however, it was less disturbing, since the largest coaches had their own convenience installed beneath the seat. For the men, the roadside offered its facilities.

At the rare houses visited by royalty, provided that the entertainment did not surpass financial comfort, the advent may have been disruptive, but it was worthwhile. It naturally gave consequence above the neighbours and a home thus graced provided gossip for a year and more. Some idea of the costs involved in a comparatively modest welcome is shown by the narrative and bills of one night's stay by George IV (when Regent) at a house in southern England. He came for the races. All the local worthies were invited as a matter of course, but their accommodation, even in a stately home, created quite a problem, as no one who lived at any distance could be expected to go home. They had to be put up for the night on hired and borrowed beds in halls and passages. Even in so princely an establishment chairs and silver, staff and waiters had to be brought in. A band was brought from London, more than a hundred miles away, as were such sweetmeats as local sources could not produce. These were, in fact, by far the largest item – nearly half the total bill – of almost five hundred eighteenth-century pounds. Wines naturally flowed, to such a degree that a mellow Highness walked the passages that night, so scaring his hostess, who was pregnant, that – we are told – fearful repercussions were prognosticated.

In all it seems that about fifty guests sat down or stood. Whether His Royal Highness gave the dispensation to sit down for an entertainment of this kind is not clear, though it is probable he did. The cost even of so comparatively modest a reception is an indication of what the Regent's own expenses must have been when entertaining hundreds of loyal lieges of the upper ranks at Carlton House.

Opposite This splendid room at Chantilly, called the salon of M. le Prince, shows the extent of decoration which might be undertaken for a special royal visit, in this case made by the boy King Louis XV and the Regent in 1722.

Painted table plan for viands set before the Prince Regent on a visit to a private house in the late 18th century.

On very special occasions, like births or victories, great cities might offer a banquet to their sovereign. These entertainments tended to be slightly less formal than palace etiquette. Here the town of Amsterdam makes such a feast. It would seem that the King and Queen are seated on high-backed chairs with their backs to the company, attended by their standing court. It is interesting to note the number and placing of the women among the others present who are seated.

More homely is another tale of straits in borrowing a state bed for Majesty to sleep in. Lent by a gracious neighbour it was taken down, transported on a farm cart and reassembled at great pother, cost and charge with all its trimmings, just before the king arrived. He took one look and had his valet set up a small truckle bed which pleased him better. Majesty, this time, was George III of England, who liked informal visiting and was most considerate of what might be involved. Perhaps, on this occasion, had he known of all the trouble that had been taken he might have slept where they designed. At another time, driving over from Windsor, he is said to have wiped his boots carefully before coming in at the front door. When his host expostulated the good king replied 'I never

bring mud into another man's house'. This time the whole staff were sent away and His Majesty was attended by host and hostess – standing all the time. He then demanded to be left alone in the house where he wandered everywhere, peering in drawers and cupboards, a pastime he enjoyed. On opening one door he found a terrified maid who had hidden herself away. Some comment like 'don't be afraid, my dear, I will not eat you', allied to the story of the mud, has been treasured in that household through the centuries.

George's courtesy in such affairs was marked and even rare. Fanny Burney tells us, almost with surprise, how George discouraged his postilions from whipping away anyone who blocked the royal path. Other cousins were not nearly so nice. Not only in this way, but in the turn-out on the route quite simple royal travel could be made into an event. Most German princes, even smaller ones, expected church bells to be rung as they passed the village street, and postilions were sent ahead to organize these tributes. Quite a number ordered a salute of cannon every time they left their town or even castle on a trip.

The most general royal travel was, of course, from one palace to another or to hunting lodges up and down the land. In view of the discomfort and confusion this entailed, the interesting thing is how much, rather than how little, these people moved about. The case of Clemens August, who had several bishoprics and other charges on his hands, may, admittedly, be a special one, but his accounts showed that he made a move several times a month. The French kings travelled almost every weekend to hunting castles in the country. Virtually all princes liked to have a summer and winter palace, even if the former were but a few miles out of town. They were so much pleasanter than all the stench and menace of the summertime in ill-drained towns. In fact Versailles, when it was the centre for the court, was almost the only all-year-round palace in the world.

Vignette from the fête book of Louis xv's visit to Strasbourg.

Government

It is absurd to attempt a review of social development in a few pages. Here we touch only on ideas that affected rulers personally. Most countries had, by the seventeenth century, inherited some form of parliament. The almost total disregard of these by absolutist monarchs was a feature of their rule. Admittedly, earlier, the findings of most of these legislatures had constitutionally only been advisory, but their deliberations commanded some respect. To princes brought up on an absolutist training the advise of a lot of self-important citizens whom they despised, was scarcely to be thought of.

So parliaments were either side-tracked or not called at all, until some crisis in affairs demanded further money, and, as writers noted, it was not so difficult for any crown, in such a climate of opinion, to pack or influence these bodies to any ends they might require. Charles II quickly had the English in control.

Any 'advice' that might effectively be taken was from ministers and favourites (posts by no means mutually exclusive), whose influence on the crown was always strong so long as they were in favour, and often almost 'absolute' where Majesty did not wish to be concerned, It was such men who ran the world behind the scenes. Yet even these might lose their place at any moment through a change of royal whim, since, whatever any prince might declare, he never could, nor did, surrender total power, unless on formal abdication.

The range and origins of the ministers in the seventeenth and eighteenth centuries is fascinating, but one common feature stands out: like Louis XIV, most kings deliberately chose their ministers without too much regard for inherited rank, but on the grounds of competence (or sometimes charm). This was part of the war against the ancient feudal aristocracy. It did not exclude a duke from becoming a minister if he was able, but most princes found it better to make a duke out of a minister who had capacity. This served a twofold purpose, in that it created opposition to the old régime and brought in newer cliques of power, whose loyalties were bound up with their sovereign's interests.

The actual contributions of the minister could be departmental or all-embracing according to his personality or that of his master.

In our period everything, from the supreme courts of justice to the visiting of a school in which he took a special interest, depended directly from the monarch personally. In this sketch by Antonio Verrio for a painting at Christ's Hospital, London, the king may be Charles II or James II. Its real significance is the weight given to such a royal visit and the comparative intimacy of such royal support.

A genius like Colbert was entrusted with everything, from war and peace to buildings and the banks. Where the pool of personnel was not so wide, people with more intellectual ability than average might find themselves drawn in to help in some position well outside their chosen field. Thus many writers became involved with politics in early eighteenth-century England. Young Goethe, in his Weimar home, was set down to a host of government activities by order of the duke. This example could be repeated many times in lesser German courts, where intellectual capacity was not endemic. Amusing and indicative too is the tale of a plot that had to be woven so that Goethe could be introduced and made respectable at court. He lacked the necessary quarterings – at least to please the duchess, who was a snob. Briefly, it involved someone having to feign illness at a card game at which the duchess was playing. As arranged, the poet was nearby and therefore called upon to make a fourth; an interruption of the game being more serious than the poet's lack of hatchments.

For a man once established as minister and favourite, the troubles as well as advantages began. There were not only the usual problems of opposition and the burdens of the office, but the fact that any projects, thoughts or ideas reached must then be sold to Majesty, whose personal reactions might well be prompted by any reason from good sense to indigestion. It is here that the intensely personal aspects of this type of government became apparent. No matter how lazy or indifferent, almost any prince was likely to argue at some point. It must have been trying enough for a busy minister to have to take up every issue with a man that he admired and whose judgment he respected, but it must have been both tiresome and discouraging to have to humour a petulant, unwilling idiot, who might be sulking because rain had interfered with his hunting, or who screamed and stamped because he thought some etiquette of reverence had been improperly performed.

Some rulers were punctilious, others might do anything, at any time, or not do them at all. Frederick the Great and Joseph II were informed and businesslike, the former instituting proper minuted reports. Others might be exact as to time but inconsiderate about what that time might be. If some liked working in the mornings, it might well be at five or six, (after going to bed at twelve or one). At such an hour, Majesty might well be 'en déshabille' or work from bed, but the minister was probably expected in full dress with orders on. Some princes liked to work at odd and unexpected hours, which meant the ministers had somehow to be there. Very often came a need for active preparation of the royal mind, to get a sympathetic hearing. Here mistresses and often queens could be invaluable. History is packed with issues that would never have matured but for their intervention.

These little troubles apart, with all but the most informed and well adapted monarchs came the dangers of outside influences or some deliberate intrigue. Whatever the cause, intrigue was almost inevitably directed against the minister. The intriguers were also likely to be 'interested', since the fruits of office were sweet indeed, and at that time it was expected that any in the garden would pluck them greedily. This meant that ministers had also to be courtiers and wait upon the entourage, as well as on the prince, or, better, seek to pack it with their nominees and placemen. This took both time and money. As a result the distribution of graft even in the highest places was phenomenal, taking almost any form from diamonds, office, orders, cash or acres, or, if Majesty agreed, that of titles which were valued highly. We must not forget that the minister himself might well be getting bribes, and acting in accordance. This whole issue was so general that any single mention must seem almost silly, yet a casual little note from an ambassador, accounting for his funds, is sinisterly informative on how to bribe the court. He told exactly who he thought was worth corrupting and who was not, and what was the price of each, from minister to backroom boy.

The letter finishes:

To this day, the 14th December, 1679, I have given to wit:

To the Duke of Buckingham, 1,000 guineas, which makes 1087l. 10s. sterling [sic].

To Mr Sidney, 500 guineas ... For the support of Mr Bulstrode 400 guineas ... To Sir John Baber 500 guineas ...

and so on. But this was pin money against what greater princes gained for making war or keeping peace or even for casting a vote for the Holy Roman Emperor. Much of the expense towards the vast palace of Pommersfelden is said to have been acquired in this way.

Those were just some of the problems involved where a single sovereign person was responsible, and those described only refer to princes who were willing, in general, to help to rule or tried seriously to do so. There were others who took no interest at all, either because they were incapable or just because they did not want to. Others again would choose to assert their authority at times, but those times might be few and far between. More than one with a more compelling interest, perhaps in hunting, but an unwillingness to delegate, went on the principle that if a letter stayed for long enough in the 'in' tray it would answer itself. Obvious confusion came as a result. Eccentrics, and they were not few, might give great trouble; one German princeling used to put his correspondence in a basket, shake the papers up and answer such as he might feel inclined, according to this lottery.

Higher in the scale of royal patronage than school-visiting came the formal presentation of royal prizes for adult intellectual activities. This bronze group with medals of the royal family supported by Religion, Piety and Cupid, was the prize for poetry won in 1714 by an Abbé Laurent Luillard in a competition in which the young Voltaire was also a candidate.

The royal arms had real significance in emphasizing rulers' penetration into every move and every act of life. The courts of justice, the coins, the weights and measures, all bore this symbol as a guarantee of rectitude. Anything remotely connected with armies, navies or the growing civil service carried the royal emblem, or at least the crown. Sometimes, as was probably the case with this poker-work coffer bearing the arms of Charles I of England, the sign could merely be an expression of loyalty towards the crown, rather than a sign of royal possession, though it might be either.

It was one thing to issue orders but another to see them carried out. In the smaller principalities – which made up the numerical majority – the problems were the same as those involved in running any nobleman's estates. In the larger kingdoms and principalities, the situation was manifestly different, and international affairs and economics depended from the actions of their governments, which meant ultimately their princes. Apart from princes of great genius, few knew much more about the detailed workings of administration than of their kitchens. Both were a complex heritage from past centuries. Most rulers were prepared to leave well alone provided that some money was forthcoming and a reasonable security prevailed.

Certainly as far as government machinery was concerned, the bewildering confusion that had come about from centuries of change, claims, concessions, rights and dues of kings and lords, priests and peasantry, towns and magistrates, needed something like a Napoleon, following on a wholesale revolution, to make effective impact. Besides, the old traditions held the thing together and the prince's circumstance as part of it. At times some obvious inefficiency would show itself and then a sense of betterment, or possibly security, even interest, might lead the ruler to attempt improvement as far as vested interests and reasonable expediency would counsel.

If there was any general move for innovation it was towards an extension of some sort of centralized civil service dependent on the crown, and this was but part of the whole, centuries-long, centralizing movement. Louis XIV planted 'Intendents', responsible to him alone, throughout the country. Those with his central justice and his secret police served to keep his interests surveyed. In Russia with its vastness, as in much of eastern Europe, the territories and estates could be so great that some autonomy for local lords was virtually inevitable if the areas were to be controlled at all. It was something that nominal allegiance should be given to a central throne even if the local conduct of affairs was arbitrary. Fortunately for the kings, the luxuries and the civilizing influences of courts appealed to noblemen of every race. In smaller, compact states, like England, control by central civil services was generally easier, at least for national issues such as finance, forces or higher justice.

As far as justice is concerned, it must be said that, any personal interest on the part of many absolutes was likely to be greater in its travesties than its administration. Secret police, imprisonment without trial, lettres de cachet, which could do anything with anybody but restore their lives, were the machinery of power. Humanitarian ideas were only just evolving in the later eighteenth century as absolutist power declined.

Even princes depended upon money, and the endless ingenuities of taxation were administered in the royal name, however farmed or gathered. The use of all direct taxes, as of rents from crown demesnes, was entirely personal and spent as Majesty might think fit. The allocations for army, navy, roads or justice, war or schools, fantastic fireworks or a hospital, a mistress or another palace were ultimately a personal decision, even if the ministers prepared the budget.

As reformers, it is in the field of economics and in the nascent social welfare and agrarian sectors that the absolutists showed some advance. The times were ripe and scientists and writers spread the word. Experiments in science and agriculture went ahead. Under royal patronage, trade was encouraged, and state transport or the roads financed. In many cases princely capital and drive encouraged the arts in the manufacture of textiles, tapestry and porcelain. These seldom paid too well, but helped provide the necessary background for the royal surroundings, which justified the patronage and intervention. In the largest countries colonial development progressed and the great trading companies of east and west were protected by the army or the navy of the state.

This rather absurd and sentimentalizing print of Emperor Joseph II inculcating agricultural enterprise illustrates as well the follies as the good intentions of these newer 'father figure' rulers. Yet they were among the best of their period and such grateful loyal tributes probably gave much encouragement in combatting obsolete, traditional bigotries and handicaps.

By the third and last quarters of the eighteenth century, thoughts on social development, as well as humanitarian ideas, began to filter through from writers and philosophers. The abolition of serfs, better education, better prisons, drainage, poor laws and a mass of other controversial issues began to enter royal heads. Many disapproved, some were just disinterested, but the better were intrigued. Such elements fell in with Christian admonition inherited from gothic times, but now the state might supplement the Church and charity. In areas like Austria and Prussia quite extensive movements were begun, with hospitals and education, especially with sequestrated churches or monastic lands. The task was often thankless, work had to push on slowly, and there was more than one recession. The opposition of vested interests might well have been expected, but it is ironical how much of the resistance came from lesser folk who would have profited from the reforms. Conservative, traditional, steeped in ancient ways so urgently supported by the church, they battled against change.

Opposition would have been inevitable even if the newly reformed administrations had been composed of angels. As it was, apart from a few on top with just a glimmer of the purpose and intentions of reform, the mass of servants of the crown were normally of limited capacity, in either mind or manner. Venality was a general practice, and as most officers were scared of those above them they bullied those below. Most had bought their little state in one way of the other and so could be relied upon to guard it with that much greater interest.

Religion

In the 17th century religion everywhere was absorbed in death and, as a corollary, damnation. By the 18th century it had become a far more comfortable affair and nowhere did this become more apparent than in the upper reaches of ecclesiastical preferment in Catholic lands. If God had made man in His own image, 18th-century man portrayed his saints in an ideal likeness of the privileged and well-born princes of the Church. Anything more superbly unlike sanctity than this exquisitely carved St Damian by Ignaz Günther would be difficult to imagine. Yet, if it is superior to most as a work of art, the attitudes of presentation were those generally adopted by the early 18th century.

This cannot be an attempt to survey the religious thought and changes through the seventeenth and eighteenth centuries or try to offer more than pointers to some ways in which the issues touched upon the monarchs of the time. As far as kings and princes were concerned the problem had two aspects: the personal beliefs of sovereigns with a care for their immortal souls, and the church or churches as an all-important social and political factor in their lands.

The seventeenth century was everywhere a period of strong religious feeling as well as controversy. Everyone felt deeply and could easily be moved to action. The Catholic revival under movements like the Jesuits was militant, while Protestants were likely to become more puritan than ever.

Yet, against this background, the deepest political issue was perhaps the fact that, just as the period saw the finish of the struggle between the barons and the crown, so it also saw, in time, the end of direct interference by the Church in temporal affairs.

At the outset monarchs as individuals could be deeply, sometimes totally involved in their religious beliefs. An almost manic religion dominated the personal approach of the Catholic sovereigns in Spain. The life of the last Spanish Hapsburg king was a fantasy of macabre behaviour as he sought to have an heir, first by one princess and then another. The practices, sanctioned by the Inquisition, fell but little short of voodoo. Yet an all-important point is that, although religion might absorb Don Carlos and the court, it remained as a personal affair between the king and God. Succession to the throne of Spain was a prize that influenced the world as well as Spain, but, in the end, the issue was decided by politics and not by the Vatican.

Charles I of England lost his throne and life partly because of his religious beliefs but more, perhaps, because he went too far (or too unwisely) along the lines his father had pursued in newer royal attitudes. The leading cardinals of France were better for their kings than for their church. In the German lands there had been one of the most appalling massacres in history – the Thirty Years War. Alignment was, ostensibly, between the rival faiths, but in fact, dynastic interests could justify alliance between

This hand *(above)*, said to be that of St John the Baptist, was an especially venerated object, even in the extensive Wittelsbach collection of relics. Acquired by King Sigismund III of Poland as booty from Moscow, it was presented to Duke Wilhelm v of Bavaria and mounted in the early 17th century. The grim message of the chasuble from Kremsmünster Abbey *(opposite)* is self-evident.

heretics – another significant feature of the royal approach to new ideas.

It was perhaps the Thirty Years War, with its awful consequences, coupled with the bigotry of incidents such as the Night of St Bartholomew that counselled greater charity in leading minds. Nevertheless, if no direct religious conflict followed after 1650, it would be a grave mistake to think that difference of faith was not profoundly influential in the progress of affairs.

Even by the eighteenth century the banner of a particular approach to God could still be raised. Such phrases as 'Bulwark against Popery' could serve a monarch or a party, but repercussions would normally be kept within the state. It was here, and in sectarian division, that a religion made its sharpest impact. The differences between a Jesuit and Jansenist, Calvinist and Lutheran, 'Church' or 'Chapel', could tear a country or upset a government but did not lead to international conflict. The situation was exploited by all kinds, from fanatics to racketeers. In its name unsavoury characters like Titus Oates could rally quite a following. Priests and people might be burned, or gruesome spectacles of Auto da Fés promoted by the keen inquisitors, but these were local things and tended to subside as the decades passed.

All this affected rulers, but on the whole most princes sought to keep themselves outside extremes, and most appreciated that, however personally distasteful, acceptance of excess was sometimes a political necessity – better a few martyrs than a civil war.

Both Catholic and Protestant rulers were ruthlessly expected to conform in so far as their thrones had been adopted by the people of one creed or the other. This was rigid in the seventeenth century, but by the eighteenth, apart from making this concession and acting prudently, the prince's contact with religion was likely to be private, and little more than a matter for his conscience – which showed increasing elasticity. Manifestly there were differences of circumstance between the Protestants who were heads of church and state, and Catholics who might still feel some allegiance to the pope, but, although old claims and controversies on rights might occasionally grumble and threats of excommunication and the like be heard, by the eighteenth century few absolutist monarchs gave them much attention. Although Holy Church, like royal mistresses, was well aware that, in an absolutist world, who ruled the monarch ruled the land, practice did not work so easily. As monarchs came to be increasingly convinced of their divine significance they proved less ready to be swayed and were resistant to any outside pressure. Most, like Charles I, conspired to make a distinction between their private and their public conscience, but managed better than he did to join the two in favour of their worldly needs.

With the utmost display of pomp and circumstance, art, cost, contrivance and magnificence the machinery of the Church was pressed into the service of absolutist princes. The coronation of Louis XIV at Reims *(right)* is scarcely a modest affair. The tomb chapel of the Medici *(below)*, with its vast over life-size figures standing on marble sarcophagi against marble panelled walls, does not betoken humility, any more than the slightly more modest, though elaborate, royal tombs of Vienna, of which this death's head *(bottom right)* wearing the Imperial crown is but a corner ornament.

On occasions when more advanced rulers sought to introduce some note of toleration they were seldom successful and certainly not popular. To achieve anything, most made use of temporal power, but far from finding a willing adoption of a liberal view, some even had to rescind what they or their predecessors had achieved.

When finally Joseph II of Austria came into real power after the death of his conservatively Catholic mother, he managed to impose toleration in his German territories and even some acceptance of the hated Jews. He even sequestrated property for more general and social purposes. But he failed in his Netherlandish dominions and that experiment contributed to his political decline. It is

The return of some slight stability in the years around 1700 encouraged an enormous development of monasticism throughout the Catholic world. Lands were acquired and huge buildings erected like this vast Benedictine establishment at Melk in Austria. Reforming princes later sought to curb this move and later still to sequestrate monastic lands.

interesting to note that even this crusading, intellectual idealist grew tired of splinter groups like Deists and enacted against them in the best despotic manner. He ruled that any, on conviction, should be summarily given 'twenty-four across the buttocks with a leather whip', the dose to be repeated as required. (This apparent piece of inconsequential thinking was justified on grounds that people such as these did not know what they were doing anyway and so deserved a whipping). On another occasion a deputation of fourteen students waited on the emperor complaining that their tutor had advised against acceptance of the orthodox biblical assessment of the age of the world. Joseph had them removed from the institution on the grounds that, if they were as stupid as that, no amount of schooling would do them any good. The tales are incidentally enlightening for what they tell us about the amount of detail into which a very hard working absolute might penetrate.

In any event, since the whole foundations of European monarchy were so bound up with Christian practice and the Christian God, it was not to be expected that a prince would openly defy religion or attempt official atheism even if he did not personally believe. A greater tolerance was the best that could be hoped for, possibly with association with societies like Freemasons. All else apart, in the period context, conformers were likely to make far better subjects than hosts of undisciplined freethinkers. That the French revolutionaries made such play of their atheism was not conviction of the merits of a world without traditional beliefs, nor entirely an hostility to church contrivance or the exploitation of the clergy. It was a blow at religion's support for traditional power.

Yet much religious association extended into official life and usually sincerely. Even the uncommitted princes sought to be baptized, as also to be married, crowned and buried with all the pomp and circumstance their church might offer. Few failed to attend their chapel regularly, perhaps more than once a day. They saw to it that their children were instructed in the proper faith. The church was part and parcel of the old traditions on which rule was based. It also kept a lot of people out of mischief. As a corollary, the priests and leaders of the church, of either faith, continued to enjoy a number of their ancient rights and privileges. The leaders of the Catholic faith, drawn normally from the highest social rank, were treated with respect. The greatest, to whom we have already referred, such as the elector bishops in Germany, had territorial rights and wealth as great as any but the largest monarchies, and are rightly considered as monarchs. So also with some Protestants, though here the priests might be of a lower caste and so not command the same respect. It can have been only rarely that a bishop or archbishop, let alone the sovereign

A baroque commentator once remarked that his contemporaries did not love God, but only feared the Devil. An all-important feature in this religion of fear was the veneration of relics—fragments of the saints and martyrs, endowed with miraculous powers, which were avidly sought after. The mediaeval traffic in them had been enormous, and baroque sympathies increased the flow. Princes were as keen as anyone and, indeed, most of the really great relics, like the True Cross, had at some time passed through royal hands. Some were reasonably portable, but baroque grandeur was very partial to full-scale corpses such as this one, dressed in ballet costume, from Waldsassen in south Germany, where it is the focus of a special feast. Said to be the body of St Maximin, it was translated from the catacombs in Rome, a source of many gifts from the highest princes of the Church. Even women were not spared and Mme de Maintenon received the full remains of St Clothilde. The Spanish royals used to borrow an especially venerated skeleton from the Church to set beside their bed on occasions of great difficulty or danger.

pontiff, received such treatment as was given by the Austrian chancellor, Prince Kaunitz, to the Pope (Pius VI). The well-intentioned prelate, recognizing Kaunitz' power, had outraged etiquette by calling personally upon the rabid anti-clerical statesman instead of seeking contact in a formal audience. He was greeted – so it is said – by Kaunitz in a dressing gown, his hand was shaken instead of kissed and in place of the long political discussion, which was the object of the visit, he was given a tour of the chancellor's very fine collection of pictures, which included several nudes. Though the emperor was perhaps unwilling to be quite so blunt himself, if he had not approved, the incident could never have occurred nor Kaunitz remained unpunished.

Everywhere something of ecclesiastical independence survived in the field of morality. It was tacitly expected that the church should take a stand if necessary, along the lines of Christian interpretation that the period understood. Even to defy the monarch from the pulpit would generally be respected if it were just, however personally unwise the act might be. This was certainly the case earlier, and the principle continued, though the phrasing of rebukes might come in more restricted terms. Everyone expected it, though few would wish it to go too far. Charles II of England appointed one bishop partly, perhaps, on the grounds of his courageous honesty when, as dean, he had refused to house Nell Gwyn, the king's mistress, who accompanied the king on a visitation. Charles respected him for it, though others might have seized his deanery.

Other bishops might be tiresome to their kings but, by the eighteenth century few tried to push their luck too far. It was understood that even where episcopal appointments were not ostensibly in royal gift they were likely to be deeply influenced by royal wishes. Sees, and even lesser places, were most important in the game of patronage and useful weapons in the armoury of rewards due for loyalty and service. Sometimes these offices were the present of the prince himself but, often, lower ranks could be distributed by ministers or mistresses as the case might be. Even quite modest cures could be a battleground in times of sharp division. Incumbents might be sacked and only reinstated on acceptance of some special oath that might be called for. The joking Ballad of the Vicar of Bray was very meaningful for any who had sought to keep a parish in the troubled times of England in the seventeenth century.

To turn again to the private and personal field. Virtually all princes, Catholic or Protestant, had been brought up in the state religion. For most, this coloured their outlook for the rest of their lives. As with any other individual the intensity of faith could vary to a great degree. At one extreme were those, like James II of

If lay princes sought apotheosis, those of the Church liked representations that were little less exaggerated. One of the greatest, the Prince Bishop Lothar Franz von Schönborn, who certainly had few rivals for the palm of patronage of art, imported the finest of Italian rococo artists, Giovanni Battista Tiepolo, to paint his soul (represented by a portrait) being born to heaven by angels, while an adoring world – all four quarters of it – looks on. The representation covers the whole of the vast ceiling of the staircase entrance to the bishop's palace at Würzburg.

These plates tell their own tale of what rococo meant to religion, from the Chelsea figure of a nun *(bottom left)* or Ignaz Günther's Guardian Angel from Munich *(opposite)* to the bishop's stalls at Regensburg *(top)* or the ivory crozier of an 18th-century bishop made by Joseph Teutschmann *(bottom right)*. It is a charming, pleasant fairy-tale, however remote from our contemporary idiom.

England or Queen Christina of Sweden, in whom the result of personal belief was so strong that they were led – when choice was forced – to leave their thrones and temporal estates to follow the doctrines they embraced. At the other end of the scale even free-thinkers like Frederick the Great paid deference to their churches, if only for political effect, though with them, as with other moderates, the influence of earlier conditioning may have been stronger than they cared to admit. Even in the eighteenth century strong elements of superstition existed everywhere and might produce most curious results at unexpected moments. It was here, if anywhere, that some political effect could still be exercized on princes. Near witchcraft was not unknown and chaplains or confessors could inspire a fear of God which might be used to advantage. With the current practices of espionage and influence of favourites it would have been most silly not to try. Both political opponents and the curia did all they could, but normally it was only in the lesser things that they succeeded.

The theatrical approach, which dominated courts and kings, fell very naturally into the daily exercize of their religious practices. Indeed, many of the very attitudes of life owed much to counter-Reformation ideas. If in the eighteenth century the climate changed from heaviness to light it was but a move from opera to the ballet. Nothing shows this better than church architecture and its decoration. Parallel with absolutist development towards benevolent dictatorship came changes in religious thought. The seventeenth-century fear had by 1800 moved to something more akin to love. In any case the deity was felt to have a particular regard for the royals' exalted station – logically enough perhaps – and they were sure that he would be prepared to make considerable allowances on their behalf. Some took advantage of the thought, but quite a number at the outset were preoccupied with the hereafter and, like their subjects, pondered about hell and death and devils. All were impressed by relics and some might turn to monkish practices of meditation in a darkened room, complete with skulls. Such macabre extravagance was very suited to the widowed or princesses left alone. Occasionally the menfolk joined them too, though normally the healthier pursuit of hunted game was adequate distraction. From an unparalleled security of wealth and rank they could enjoy the frisson of an hour-long thundering on death, damnation and the rest convinced, perhaps, that such things were not for likes of them.

By the eighteenth century, though personal admonishment might be no whit less necessary, such direct threats were out of date. Confessors could do more. Established courts and princes went their own ways and any comment was expected to conform within the finer etiquettes. Sermons might be quite as long, but

phrased with better taste. Chapels were attended and good works done. In Catholic lands the monasteries and nunneries for princely families were no less popular – indeed they flourished – but the skulls were put back in the charnel house, the scourge replaced by needlework. Though it did not always have the same exuberance as in south Germany, rococo was introduced everywhere. The same theatrical approach informed the mind and matter of religion for the privileged. In the great German sees, which were always reserved for the very highest families, incumbents used their place and emoluments to further their dynastic or their architectural dreams. Never has church building or church decoration prospered better than when guided by these highly cultivated princes.

At the courts, religion served for yet another, and at times more serious play. Here even Innocence and Piety might play a lead. They did exist, though possibly more often where the former had prepared the latter's way. Prayer, sometimes undertaken in what we might regard as attitudes of over-affectation, with moans and

Scarcely less magnificent than the lay structure, though of rather more modest dimensions, was the court chapel attached to the bishop's palace at Würzburg.

If Günther's saint *(right)* can moan and groan in prayer like any pious prince, the French king's painter, Carle van Loo, favoured more ordered behaviour from those attending Our Lord in adoration *(left)*. Care is even taken that the family appears rather as carpenter's kin than as persons of quality.

groans, tears and rolling eyes, served to give strength and resignation where the cares of royalty were felt too much. If the idiom was not ours, it could be quite sincere and genuine. All this could be achieved with absolute conviction, since almost all believed that everything existed by conscious intervention of the 'Will of God'. The catechisms emphasized that part about the 'Station unto which it shall please God', etc. Thus few performers felt the slightest shiver of reproach or ever questioned their comparative advantages or thought too much of starving masses – certainly no more than the West does today. The problem, then, as now, was not immediately soluble. If the masses sometimes rose in the extremest need, few ever thought of their position as a sign of disorder in temporal affairs. So court religious services could go on, as all the other aspects of their life, a cultivated, urbane, civilized affair in which unpleasant things were, as far as possible, set aside.

Only the atheists who read the works of M. Voltaire might whisper in the wings. It was regretable that some wore coronets and one or two were even crowned. Yet even they could not disturb the general dream of the Almighty as a kindly, bearded, rosy-cheeked old gentleman who could perhaps get a little cross, set well above rococo clouds attended by enchanting angels and most elegant and pretty interceding saints. The whole scene was comparable to those apotheoses where the sovereign persons, also always good and kindly, sat among the ancient gods.

One, at least, of the old Christian virtues remained strong: in addition to establishing schools of art, educational foundations, and similar institutions on what we have referred to as a 'national' scale, the old-time personal charities and usages went on as cozened by the Christian faith. Princes did build hospitals out of their own purse (as far as such a distinction could be made) and wrote their names in golden letters on the front. They did endow schools and scholarships. These things were done not only from faith or charity, but as insurance for their souls. The pious continued to support the churches, convents, almshouses or monasteries, taking a direct personal interest as well as merely giving money. They would visit them, they would attend on founder's days and personally follow up the welfare of the institution that they patronized. Even as children, princes and princesses were expected to subscribe and give their pocket money and at times their help.

In most countries more intimate, traditional, even almost pagan, ceremonies were still continued. An example, 'Touching for the King's Evil', was a regular practice in England, and similar customs persisted in other lands. Like the ceremony of coronation such elements could stress the instinct of people everywhere to vest their rulers with divinity. As far as the vaunted twentieth century is concerned, the adulation given to dictators, however terrifying it may seem, varies in focus but not in essence from tradition.

At no point in religion was dynastic pride really abandoned, whether in the silver container for a Wittelsbach heart *(above)*, bequeathed to the prince's favoured church, or the embroidered arms on a prayer-book cover *(below)*, said to have belonged to Charles I of England.

The Armed Forces

While we cannot attempt to outline the military history of the seventeenth and eighteenth centuries, we can examine attitudes of the age to armies and navies as they affected the rulers personally.

On this point our commentator of 1694 succinctly remarked that 'A considering English traveller will find by experience, that at present nothing is so generally studied by *Sovereign Princes* than the Arts of War'. In perspective, the emphasis on the 'Arts' of war might have a wider significance for us than the author intended at the time. The seventeenth and early eighteenth centuries saw great changes in military tradition. On the one hand came the evolution of trained standing troops commanded by professionals – albeit mainly aristocrats – and on the other an increasing detachment by the sovereign in person from direct association in the field.

Obviously all princes depended for aggression or defence upon their troops, but the pattern of affairs had developed by the eighteenth century so that only a handful of these potentates was in a state to aggress or to defend on any scale at all. These great sovereigns conducted national – if still dynastic – wars. The rest, apart from hiring mercenaries, kept out of trouble or made such token gestures of alliance as they deemed expedient. They had little or no opening for declaring wars on their own initiative. Yet this did not stop them keeping little armies more or less as things to play with as a change from hunting. For many princelings this was their greatest diversion and in this game even the greater cousins would join delightedly.

The extent to which this passion developed is especially well illustrated in the German states. Even the smallest princes would play as far as (and even further than) their purses would allow. The Landgraf of Pirnesen, for example, one way or another involved more than three-quarters of his population (of a few thousand) to play soldiers. Naturally enough, this led to the ruin of his economy.

Such potentates as Frederick William were obsessed by their game of soldiers. For his crack troops he would spend as much as others did upon their opera or works of art. He particularly favoured the very tall and had a contract with the Tsar for a hundred or so Russian giants to be handed over annually. He was not

By the end of the 17th century it was becoming the exception rather than the rule for absolute monarchs to attend on the battlefield in person. This did not prevent them enjoying all the glamour of war and victory and using every gesture of baroque rhetoric to show themselves as triumphant leaders. Here William III of England prances at the head of his troops after a victory, perhaps that at the Boyne.

This sentry box, designed for Catherine the Great by her Scottish court architect James Cameron, almost reaches the limit in make-believe and playing soldiers.

even above border raiding for a particularly desirable specimen. Other princes used to send him them as presents. Lothar Franz von Schönborn, the great builder at Würzburg and Pommersfelden, recounts how he had once been offered two boys from the country, whom he had refused. He very much regretted this when he learned that they were 'extra long and would have done as Prussian grenadiers. I would gladly have had something extra large in that line to send as an especial present to the King in Prussia. I am sure I would have had two nice original pictures or something of the sort in return.' Iron discipline and all that went with it played its part, but the specials cut much figure in the land. They were dressed up, paraded, pampered, petted and admired, like fat stock at a show. The swaggering soldier bully of comedy and caricature must have been very much in evidence among officers as well as other ranks.

The princes loved these animated toys and used them with a full rococo sense of theatre. They rose early when they drilled their troops, made parades on any possible occasion, designed new uniforms, and even pressed them into service for the opera 'crowds'. When these real-life dolls were set in pretty patterns at garden fêtes, or ranged up steps and round the galleries at balls, such public demonstrations also served to warn the public that some private guards were there. In the greater states the army had to be prepared for use at home as much as in any war abroad, but the tinier collections might at least ward off a burglar or an importunate foreigner, as in the case of James Boswell. He has an amusing tale (in the story of his Grand Tour of 1764), of his arrest in the territories of Prince of Zerbst, 'a strange wrongheaded being. He has got his troops, forsooth, to the number of 150 foot and 30 horses, and, during the last war, took a fancy that the King of Prussia was coming to attack him. So, he put in readiness his little battery of cannon, and led out his 180 to make head against the armies of Frederick'. It was one of these 'blackguard dogs' who sought to arrest Boswell. The tale does have some wider significance for the story of lesser principalities. If the gesture against Frederick seems pathetically comic, it could have been made in earnest, had there been the need. These princes and their men had courage, and in their tiny cosmos did not always see the world outside as all that much greater than themselves. Expressive too of the theatrical side of these minuscule arrays is Boswell's comment on the 'sentinels with sentry boxes painted in lozenges of different colours, like the stocking of Harlequin'. This 'diverted' the passing Scot, but a fellow national, James Cameron, seems to have accepted the theatricality most amiably; as he himself designed a sentry box for Catherine the Great.

Naturally the few great national monarchs had their serious

armies which they used in battle, often in appalling circumstances. As, with increasingly rare exceptions, the sovereign no longer went to war in person, it was the political aspect which really touched him. Occasionally, as bravery was still admired, a king or prince might make a token gesture in the field – George II was the last English king to do so – and his popularity advanced as a result. But on the whole, so active a participation did not accord with absolute exclusiveness. Nor, in usual circumstances, did it help towards the most effective conduct of the war, unless, as with Charles XII or Frederick the Great, the reigning prince was also a commander of great genius. Such men naturally and instinctively led armies and had complete control of military affairs, which could be a mixed blessing for their peoples.

Although no sovereign renounced his right as ultimate commander of his forces, the greater number wisely left the conduct of the battles in more expert hands and limited attendance to the grand reviews and rallies after victory, to claim as theirs what other men had won. If the victory was good enough and booty adequate, royal stock might rise and it was silly not to take advantage. Besides, many could persuade themselves that but for the direction from behind the scenes the war might never have been won. Sometimes indeed this was the case, but sometimes it was in spite of royal intervention that the general achieved victory. Certainly, as Marlborough well knew, few fields were wider open to intrigue than those behind the backs of absent marshals.

There was always a rather special sentimental link between the crown and forces, since by tradition all the oaths were taken to the crown itself. Allegiance was to His Majesty (addition of 'and country' to 'For king' did not come in till later centuries). Perhaps all this appealed more happily to those who were recruited voluntarily rather than to the press-ganged or those taken from the gaols. The romantic element, so popular in prints of soldier man or sailor boy, did, in fact, exist in life. The qualities of manliness and adventure were admired and could still draw young recruits who made perhaps the better soldiers. The rest accepted, since, as a contemporary remarked, it made so little difference 'to change one slavery for another' and at least there might be food, and sometimes pay and booty, a pretty uniform or even village recognition.

Such an appeal was obviously likely to have a greater draw to aristocrats than farm boys. Their circumstances in the field or on parade were reasonably good. The métier of officer was their exclusive right and held up as ideal. Few lacked stark courage and many liked to show it. To look handsome in a smart uniform was just as pleasant in the eighteenth century as at any other time. Besides, for many there was little choice except the service or rotting on distant and diminishing estates.

Even a very brave king like Louis XIV, who did not hesitate to join the field himself, enjoyed the panoply of war enormously. Here, although in this particular case the King had not himself been fighting, he is shown by the artist A. van der Meulen making a triumphal entry, attended by a vast court and all the women, into the newly captured town of Arras in 1667.

Even princes were affected by this call. More than one monarch slept upon his camp bed and awoke to martial sounds, even among later kings who took no active part in the campaigns. Most liked to have seen some service when young as a proof of courage and ability to rough it, and proudly added military reminiscence to their hunting tales, even if they had never seen a shot fired in earnest nor dined off anything other than the finest silver plate when on manoeuvres.

If the reigning princes or those next in line were likely to be kept at home, more distant heirs like brothers, cousins, uncles, nephews, younger sons and such were often given high command and sent about the royal affairs. Almost as a complement to the new theories, such associations helped retain the best of the old tradition of a personal association with the crown. It also gave these relatives some purpose that might justify emoluments. They were not always an advantage, for although they were usually supposed to be under the direction of the general in command, the obedience of such high-born staff could be as unpredictable as their ability.

More than one battle was lost because some royal prince was late or saw fit to charge off on his own, with possibly spectacular effect but with ruin to the strategy. Prince Rupert has upon occasion borne the blame for losing battles in this way, and so the

war, and ultimately his father's throne. There was, of course, another side to the picture. Some generals of royal blood were first-rate soldiers, like Maurice de Saxe or Prince Eugen. In such cases they were of great advantage since their rank upheld the basic principle of rule by royalty. In this case bastardy was welcome.

Within the regiments, since almost all were officered by nobles, or at least by gentlemen, none could take offence at a reprimand from one of equal or of even better birth. In the context of the times such considerations were of paramount importance in maintaining discipline. But unfortunately for their troops, many royal officers in command were not capable. Even the pure figurehead, as imagined by the nineteenth century, could interfere and intervene with mixed advantage.

The navies on the whole were less likely to be visited royally or to suffer interference. Few capitals were near the sea and, apart from occasional monarchs like Charles II of England or Peter of Russia, hardly any had any leanings in this direction and most felt a greater sympathy for the soldiers they could play with every day than for crews and ships that were away for months and years on end, protecting trade routes or acquiring colonies. An occasional review to encourage such morale as could be expected from a press-ganged crew might still find its place from time to

The exquisite Sèvres vase of which a detail of the decoration is shown here was bought by Louis xv in 1759. Few objects bear more telling witness to the fairy-story transformation that could be applied to blood, sweat, toil, tears, brutality and horror to make them agreeable to kings and queens, princes and princesses.

185

We have seen that even the horrors of war had to be presented decoratively before princely eyes. Many princes took an active part in the design of uniforms for their troops and this drawing by Parrocel *(right)* is one of a group showing the elaboration of such dress. The General Adam Ludwig Levenhaupt had the silversmith I. G. Eben cast a pretty silver plaque *(opposite top left)* to record all his victories for Charles XII of Sweden; this was made in Riga in 1705. Ships had long been pressed into decorative service, like this ivory cup *(far right)*. One of the greatest generals of his day, Prince Eugen was also one of the great artistic patrons. Even his severely practical sword, cane and baton *(opposite bottom left)* were most beautifully and restrainedly decorated.

time or at a threat of war. By the same token aristocratic leadership, though equally desirable in principle, tended in the case of the navies to be subordinated to some capacity and training. In the last resort ships were difficult to manage and expensive to replace so that an incompetent manoeuvre could be a good deal more costly on sea than land. The lords high admiral might be direct appointments by the crown, and, as in the case of the Duke of York, be royal and play an active part in battle. Most were content either to be engaged on the administrative side or treat the post as just another sinecure.

Whether army or navy the chronic issue for all monarchs was to pay the bills. One or other service, or sometimes both, were often in a desperate state of inefficiency and disrepair until a crisis came to rescue them and national emergency diverted some resources to their needs.

The most cynical and disreputable practice among quite a lot of princes was that of hiring out their troops as mercenaries – a very different issue from that of an individual hiring himself for pay. How profitable this extension of the hobby could be was strikingly emphasized in the case of the Markgraf of Anspach who sold some two and a half thousand head of troops to England for over a quarter of a million pounds. They were largely impressed material, gaol sweepings and the like, but as more than half returned to him in reasonably good order some years later – in 1783 – he had little to complain about. As his chancellor remarked, these men had been conscripted for the good of their country and as chronic financial embarrassment was the country's gravest trouble they had nobly performed the purpose for which they were designed.

Ranking high in the royal association with military affairs were the schools for officers which they established almost everywhere, particularly in the late eighteenth century. Originally they were designed to create a corps d'élite. Drawn normally from the sons of poorer noble families, the cadets who had the requisite quarterings were seriously trained as officers. It was hoped in this way to inculcate a standard of usefulness more reliable than that of some boy who had been bought his regiment and had little more knowledge than how to behave or ride a horse. It also served to get a group conditioned in loyalty to the crown from those supposedly grateful for the free training and education they had received.

While the strictly military bias and discipline was maintained in the curriculum, most of these academies quickly became established as centres of privileged education, with the idea that the graduates might well take up other positions for their country or the crown. Frederick's development in Prussia served both purposes and it also offered an alternative to the Versailles method of breaking noble power. By making a military career the most highly honoured outlet for a nobleman, Frederick quickly turned the children of his turbulent northern barons into regimented and conditioned slaves. After a period at one of these terrifying establishments, if they could think at all, they could only do so along the lines of blind obedience to orders and their king. As he happened to be a brilliant soldier and a highly admired individual, this allegiance may not have been so hard to hold.

For the 17th and 18th centuries, while delight in killing things was paramount, dressing up to go killing things was very much part of it. Each hunt had its own special uniforms and details and everything underwent the most elaborate decoration, from the stocks and locks of guns to ancillary equipment such as this green velvet hunting burse or the finely carved ivory powder flask.

Pastimes

With courts and suites numbering hundreds of people most of whom had twenty-four hours in the day and 365 days in the year with nothing purposeful to occupy them, something had to be done to keep them out of mischief. Indeed the whole political purpose of this development of the court would have been defeated if they were not. Also princes themselves when they were not working (which was often much of the time), at the table or in bed needed some diversion.

The rounds of distraction provided for them were perhaps the most elaborate and expensive per head per annum that there had ever been, certainly since classical times. Outside, hunting took pride of place with the men, often to the exclusion of everything else. Shooting and, to a very much smaller degree, fishing were indulged. Such slight diversions as picnics in toy houses, boating on lakes or taking the air in little carriages, which make such charming pictures, were largely engaged upon by women. If they appear accompanied by men it was as hangers on that most of them joined these rather dull pursuits. Indoors, theatre, ballets, opera and concerts vied with gambling and balls for general favour. The performances might be held outside on special occasions and be accompanied by feasting and fireworks. Meals assumed an important place for the ritual and settings, plate and decorations rather than the food that might be eaten. Gallantry joined reading as a means of passing the time. Intellectual conversation was rare in royal precincts.

Of all those diversions the chase was by far and away the greatest in most royal eyes. Hunting in the seventeenth and eighteenth centuries was on a scale that makes any of today's activities seem almost absurd. Anything that ran, flew, swam or moved was potential game, though by general consensus the bigger were the better and one only took the lesser when the former were in short supply. Hecatombs of beasts were slaughtered every day to keep the privileged amused, especially on the continent, where bigger game was far more plentiful than in England.

Stags were, in general, the most favoured quarry, with boar as second. Wolf and even bear might serve in remote places though these were becoming rare in populated areas. Hares and foxes were

Even an opponent of stag hunting could not deny that J. F. de Troy has made a picture of the greatest beauty from the scene. The force and vigour of the sketch serves to emphasize the vigour of the beasts and hard intensity of the men.

Few sporting pictures show in such detail the full turn out of a royal hunt. Here V. A. Cignaroli's picture shows the entrain setting out for a day with the Turin court.

pursued when larger animals could not be found, though these were rather despised in the best continental circles, unless as a quarry for the falcons.

The main feature which differentiates these baroque hunts from blood-sports of today was the scale of massacre and the motivation – which was sheer and uninhibited delight in killing. Death had its attraction for its own sake and was of prime importance. The struggle between hound and beast and the blood itself found far more favour then than now – or than today would ordinarily be admitted. While something of the excitement of the chase, the comradeship, and even the air and exercize which lie at the root of sport was understood, it was the flow of blood and stink of death that were exciting to the seventeenth- and eighteenth-century mind.

This aspect is underlined by the fact that although 'parforce' hunting (that is, hunting on horseback and in pursuit of the quarry over countryside) was the most popular form, everyone was prepared to indulge and enjoy sitting in butts while hundreds of driven beasts were herded round an enclosure to be watched as they fought with dogs or were shot at as they passed. It was inhospitable not to give a guest as many animals as he could wish and three or four hundred stags for a short princely visit was not considered more than reasonable. Less would have been mean and more was frequent. Six thousand head of game including two thousand six hundred boar were said to have been produced for a visit of the Grand Duke Paul of Russia to the court of Württemberg.

In all this blood-letting the women often took as active a part as the men, certainly in the earlier period before swooning and more genteel attitudes were called for and women had become known as the 'fairer sex' or some other such euphemism. Queen Anne of England, for example, was as passionate as any and when she grew too vast to ride followed the chase in a specially constructed chay. Most princesses, even if they did not follow from the start, were expected to turn up later in a coach and watch the rituals of death and dismemberment.

Next to pursuit by dogs, falconry was perhaps the most in favour. Here it was chiefly heron and hare that died in this rather more refined and traditional sport, though other birds and beasts might also fall. The practice was still mainly central European though it no longer had the same following as in the middle ages, when an emperor could himself write the definitive treatise and claim that such hunting was a release from the 'fatigues of administration for the great and noble while it provided work for the poor in their employ'.

Yet for hunting in general the words were just as applicable in baroque times, except that the great and noble had not usually

laboured quite as hard as mediaeval princes might have had to do. Certainly, the hordes of huntsmen, grooms, wardens, game keepers, farriers, dog men, beaters and the rest made up a formidable industry in eighteenth-century terms. The depredations of the game on the meagre cultivations of the poor, or the damage done by callous hunting parties riding over fields were just another burden on the peasants' backs. Savage game laws still protected every aspect of the owner's sport whether he was great or small and their administration was still in the hands of local justices who were, of course, invariably the owners or their tools.

Shooting, other than at big driven game, did exist, but the slowness of the firearms normally favoured a sitting rather than a moving target. Nonetheless it served as sport if there was nothing else to do. A young prince visiting the Grand Duke of Tuscany is credited with shooting at birds on a palace tapestry when rain prevented outdoor exercize. Except in vast organized massacres of driven game, shooting was a diversion in which by the eighteenth-century royal standards there was insufficient blood about. On occasions at some northern courts everyone went out in boats when the young swans or geese and ducks were swimming round before their wing feathers had grown long enough for them to fly. They were then shot by the thousand, 'and the water coloured with their blood'. This was regarded as most amusing and at least the results of these massacres provided down for pillows, though the flesh was 'good for nothing', we are told.

As the illustrations show, most elaborate inventions might be created to vary the monotony, as with the Bucentaure converted into a butt on the Starnberg See. The cupola parapet at the exquisite Amalienburg was designed as a stand for shooting driven pheasants. Animals were even driven on to stage set scenes with mazes and steps the better to add to their confusion; and thus was the fun of massacre increased. Grenades could be used as bullets

18th-century hunting was a vigorous, even vicious, affair, in which the massacre of beasts was what counted and all kinds of ingenious variations were thought up. In this case a version of the Ducal barge from Venice – the Bucentauro – was reconstructed on the Starnberg See, just south of Munich, where it could be used for any pleasures, such as watching fireworks, listening to a concert or as a butt for shooting driven game. As can be seen in this model, the ship was of a considerable size and could take two or three hundred staff and guests.

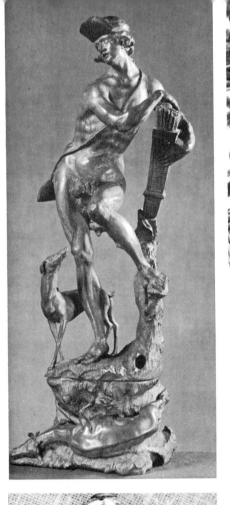

Not unnaturally the most favoured
sport of all was pressed into the
service of art. If the exquisite
German sword and hunting belt in
green enamel *(left and far left
bottom)* might be regarded as
rather unpractical accoutrement
for the chase, the decorative
motifs were taken from the birds
and beasts pursued. The influence
of the hunt on pure works of art
is seen in the enchanting boxwood
figure of a huntsman *(far left top)*
or the beautiful model of Diana
carved by the great rococo artist
Ferdinand Dietz *(right)*. The
architect Cuvilliés' debt to all
sports, here *(below right)* fishing,
is manifest in every detail of
decoration of the most wonderful
of all hunting lodges, the
Amalienburg, near Munich. All
the objects on these pages date
from around the second quarter of
the 18th century.

and any means like fire and smoke employed to make the quarry move.

Diversions in ways of maiming, were, of course, thought up. One of the more appreciated in Germany was fox tossing. Here the terrified beast was made to run the gauntlet of a line of paired off courtiers, men and women. These held the ends of a narrow net which lay on the ground. The sport was to see which pair was quickest at jerking the net just as the fox passed over, thus hurling it into the air. It was great fun particularly if the wretched animal broke its leg or back when falling and especially if it ran under a lady's skirt for shelter.

It is particularly in things like this that we see how different was the outlook of the period from that today. The mentality that they indulged in many sports was frankly cruel, rough and tough and such as we might expect in a vitiated schoolboy rather than an adult of the leading class. Whether this is a sign of decadence or of advance in us is quite another matter. However much we might be amused by the spectacle, few would not regard it as a sign of grave disturbance of the mind if we were to see our monarch or our president jumping up and down in the bowels of a fallen stag, as James I used to do. We might even be a little discomforted at some of the sturdy horseplay which was often associated with the chase. The practice at Fredericksborg was to hold a mock court in the royal presence on returning from the hunt to adjudge on any who had committed a 'transgression against the known laws of hunting that day'.

The accused is generally found guilty; and then two gentlemen lead him to the stag, and make him kneel down between the horns turning down his Head with his Buttocks up, and remove the skirts of his coats, which might intercept the blows; then comes His Majesty, and with a small long wand, gives the offender some lashes on his Posteriours whilst in the meantime the Huntsmen, with the Brass-Horns, and the Dogs with their loud openings, proclaim the King's Justice ... The whole scene affording diversion to the Queen, Ladies and other spectators.

Such uninhibited public fun was in the eighteenth century the rule rather than exceptional.

Such sportive ceremonies might express the ease and informality that hunting could provide, but they also emphasize the special rules and etiquettes which each hunt had. If the courts had elaborate provision for special costumes or behaviour, the hunts were no less exacting, and any infringement was regarded by many as far more heinous than neglect of normal Christian practice.

The gentler forms of killing, like fishing, might find favour but were not so much pursued by kings. They were held as rather bourgeois sports. Similarly, games like bear-baiting or cock-

In 1756 Johann Heinrich Tischbein the Elder decorated an entire room in the Hesse hunting lodge of Wabern near Fritzlar with scenes of the court out falconing. These are now in the Heron Hall of Schloss Fasanerie at Fulda. There are few such accurate and complete records showing every detail down to the formalities at the end, where the Princess gives her approval and the noble company takes refreshment in a special decorated tent.

Souvenirs of the chase abounded and, in every castle, halls and passages proclaimed the fortunes of succeeding generations in acquiring odd or special heads. Sometimes these were curiously mounted, but few went so far as to create all the furniture as well as decorations out of antlers as in this 18th-century room in the castle of Ohrada, Czechoslovakia. It must be admitted that the blend of taste and eccentricity has been quite successful.

fighting were mainly popular. On a festive occasion, rather eccentric individuals at very small courts might join the populace to see the fun, but on the whole these more intimate associations were not really quite in keeping with the newer image of a Highness. For renaissance princes they had been all right, but then renaissance princes were a part of – not totally removed from – their subjects.

Outside bloodsport, few games counted. Of ball games and such, tennis (indoor) or billiards were those most favoured. Others, like embryo golf or cricket, had not yet penetrated into palace life expect in nursery forms. On the whole, exertion, except on a horse, was found unseemly.

It is curious that outside England, horse racing does not seem to have been regarded as essentially the sport of kings. In Britain from Stuart times it had always been royally supported and monarchs went to pains to attend the leading meetings, founding many of the courses themselves. They gave cups and prizes and wagered too, and some took an interest in bloodstock.

So popular was hunting that in many cases the whole court life was adapted to the chase. Many monarchs rose very early – five or six was not unusual. They did so not to leave for the hunt at that hour but to get their work done so as to be free to go when the light and scent were right. This was often later in the day, and, since the game was artifically provided, the hunt could start at Majesty's convenience. Many a minister found his life embittered (or made easier at normal hours) because his master would prefer his hunting to affairs and so expect attendance at dawn or midnight to make up for lost time. And of course rain on a hunting day could so spoil the princely temper as to make proper attention or civil argument extremely tricky if he was called on to pay heed to government.

For the twentieth century it is perhaps the ancillary developments from eighteenth-century hunting that are more important than the mountains of dead animals. To pursue this game the greater princes built special hunting lodges both near their castles and on properties around which fresh game might be collected when one ground had been exhausted. Some of these like Falkenslust near Brühl or the Amalienburg attached to the Nymphenburg, the summer palace near Munich, are among the most exquisite architectural achievements of the time. As a recent writer noted, no period had a greater facility for sublimating that 'stink of urine' so inseparable from blood sport and through their aesthetic to reach a synthesis of art and death. Since hunting was the first interest and the first preoccupation of most princes, every association with the chase readily came to be transformed into art. This might be directly connected, as in the special uniforms that had to be designed, or work on the knives and trappings, belts and horns or even dog collars that were made attractive. In turn references to venary were adapted for every conceivable medium. Not only painters and sculptors but stucco workers, jewellers, gold- and silversmiths, engravers, porcelain modellers, tapestry workers and every other decorative craftsman sought inspiration in one or other branch of hunting.

To us the lesser outdoor pastimes seem very tame, as indeed they were. Most were designed for the women. Driving about in cabriolets or sailing a boat were scarcely more exhilarating than the endless little innocent picnics in the woods where grown-ups played at blind man's buff, or battledore and shuttlecock as readily as children.

Certainly by the eighteenth century the passion for building little houses like the hunting lodges had reached a happy outlet in the *bergeries,* and exotic little farms and tea houses that princesses set up in their parks as goals for an afternoon's walk, where some collation might be served or where they might pretend, for a moment, to be ordinary persons with their intimates, instead of royalty on show at court.

As the escapist romanticism of the eighteenth century developed, such play houses increased in popularity. They made it possible for the attitudes of the theatre to be lived in real life – or as real as these players ever had it. To read Ossian or Werther in a grotto; to make butter in a fancy dairy, to pose in a classical temple as Vesta or Venus, discussing the latest novel, exchanging gossip or just simpering platitudes, whiled away an hour or two before it was time to dress up again to go back on parade.

Hunting motifs decorated more intimate objects, from snuff boxes or jewellery to firedogs or candlesticks. On this example a Chelsea porcelain modeller has used a continental model with a boar, rather surprising since the animal was virtually extinct in England by the 18th century.

Indoor Amusements

For indoor amusements the opera and ballet, music and the stage, perhaps in that order, vied with gambling and balls for popularity. There is no place here to attempt a survey of the technical and artistic developments of the baroque theatre, but it is pertinent to stress two points. First, that the stage revival was directly due to the courts and at least until the eighteenth century was almost entirely dependent on them for support. Secondly, to understand the full significance of the theatre at the time, it is essential to appreciate how far it had become a part of life. In the words of a recent writer 'it is no accident that stage scenes and the new absolutism rose together'. Kings and courtiers alike were playacting with every ritual of their existence whether with the costumes, their postures, etiquettes, behaviour, their affectations or even speech. The rooms and palaces were deliberately scenic and designed to enhance the whole vast artificial make-believe which had become reality. By the same token the events about the court were continuously being brought into actual stage performances. Special works were written for formal state occasions, apposite pieces were chosen for particular circumstances. Lines were adapted, both in serious plays as well as comedies, to suit some current topic which the whole community would recognize. Compliments could readily be paid to visitors of eminence by words from gods and heroes on the stage. So indeed could criticism, and for this censorship and licences had very soon evolved. In fact, the theatre had come to be an extension of the court about it, not simply a change from dancing, gambling or the table.

If court sponsorship was responsible for the promotion it was also responsible for the tenor of the new development. Some fantasy and panache coupled with a rude philosophy and bawdy had always had their place with entertainers, even in the mystery plays. Onto this modest heritage the princes grafted lavish spectacle and classical discoveries. The whole of their world took to it and soon a new approach, especially in opera and ballet, evolved from this inheritance. Even by the later 1600s the available material was quite extensive, and if, at times, quality was lacking, there was quantity enough that could be furbished up. By 1700 the repertoire of operas alone amounted to several hundreds.

The Austrian royal party at the theatre, a painting from the Schönbrunn series of the marriage of Joseph II.

Above The art world was truly international. Here the model, George Frederick Handel, and the sculptor, L. F. Roubiliac, were aliens in England patronized both by an alien king and a native burgher, who bought the statue for the Vauxhall Gardens, where in the 1730s music and bawdy could meet on equal terms.

Opposite This mid-18th-century Frankenthal porcelain figure of Oceanus by Konrad Linck shows all the extravagance of ballet costume at the time.

Every great prince supported these things to the full extent of his ability and some beyond their purse, for the costs could be prodigious. Naturally the opera and ballet were likely to be most expensive and need the most attention. Then, as today, subvention was essential, for in addition to the companies and stars came all the other liabilities involved, the scenery and costumes, cleaners, stage hands and even lighting, which was as expensive as it might be dangerous. There was also need of good technicians and machinery; the best of baroque theatre was nothing if not theatrical and changed its scenes and mounted its effects as no one could today, except, perhaps, in state-supported ballet.

Lady Mary Wortley Montagu was told that thirty thousand pounds had been expended on just one court performance in Vienna with most lavish costumes, stage effects of fire and water, boats and all the rest. This does not seem unlikely when quite modest private shows by wealthy amateurs could readily cost two or three thousand pounds, even if the performances lasted only two or three nights.

Some savings might be made by using talent locally available and few court painters were not recruited for painting scenery or at least designing it. The court musicians would provide the music. Footmen or the prettier huntsmen might occasionally be set about to help out crowds or decoration, and for this the soldiery were useful too, since at least they had been taught to walk with order and precision.

At poorer courts such shifts were naturally inevitable and in the case of the smallest a good deal of tolerance must often have been called for. In the spirit of the times it was no doubt forthcoming; distractions were not so readily available and the sense of audience participation may well have been far greater than today.

The almost universal eighteenth-century practice of amateur theatricals would have helped in this. If any court of note could count on two or even three professional performances a week when in residence, still, somehow, somewhere in the ambience, Royal Highnesses and noble persons would be conning lines or even writing them for yet another evening's entertainment. This dilettante practice was by no means limited to plays. Since ballet, at least till later times, did not depend so much on virtuosity and soloists, amateurs could take a part in ordered miming. Whatever else had been left out of education, grace and deportment had always been included. Besides, the opportunities for dressing up were limitless and that was something all could enjoy. Even opera was staged by amateurs, though not so frequently, as voices must be born as well as trained. Yet even here, anyone at court with any gift at all would have been schooled, if only because they had nothing else to do.

Two 18th-century princely theatres. The one *(top)* is at Česky Krumlov in Bohemia, the other *(bottom),* created by Cuvilliés for the Residenz at Munich, is the ultimate in rococo decoration, dating from the mid-century.

The tradition of the masques and sumptuous pageants which renaissance princes so enjoyed and in which the company could pass whole days in fancy dress as gods and goddesses was very strong, and no doubt helped to prepare the way for the formal acting of the later time.

The touring companies on whom the bulk of all performances outside the greatest capitals depended might be pretty rough, and being often almost family affairs demand much doubling up, with actors and actresses coping with effects and even scenery. Goethe tells us of a time when he was acting impresario for his duke in Weimar, of someone having to mime in double on the opera stage, while the lead sang in the wings. She was so drunk that, although still singing, she could not be relied upon to stand. Such events must have been quite frequent. Most of these touring companies were French or Italians, who passed from town to town or court to court. Decent actor managers rose quite high in public recognition as did the leading actresses – who, then, might join that calling with another, older one – and the players, on the whole, could live a far less straitened life than, for example, many lesser clergymen. In the bigger companies of thirty or forty people giving regular performances and normally based upon a court or capital some semblance of regular employment could be gained.

At first no one at the court thought of paying and the seats were just a part of royal largesse. Plays were attended like any other court function both to see and to be seen. The position and placing of each individual in the audience meant quite as much to most of them as the performance. As many were of limited intelligence the lavish staging and effects were of more concern than intellectual content in the play. This partly accounted for the popularity of opera and ballet, which also cut out something of the language barrier.

In the early days, performances took place in a hall within the palace, or nearby, which had been adapted for the purpose. Sometimes more respectable burghers might get in by payment, or the 'royal' company might go to town and play for money. This helped with the expenses. By the late seventeenth century in larger capitals and by the eighteenth almost everywhere a change came in. While special, well-equipped private theatres were still part of every princely home, public theatres started up within the town or near the palace. These were supported to a great or less degree by the princes. They would arrive by coach, and were arranged in sumptuous boxes kept at the disposal of the court. Many exist today, as at Bayreuth or the Residenz at Munich, which are still active centres of international fame. Drottningholm can even stage original scenery and effects, as also, when restored, may Česky Krumlov.

So great was the vogue for theatre that elaborate temporary installations might be set up for special visits. When Clemens August found he had to spend three months at Morgentheim, the castle of his Teutonic Order, he had a special theatre built inside the courtyard and engaged both French and Italian troupes of fifty persons to perform.

In certain towns, like Venice or London, there were populations of sufficient wealth and interest to keep up theatres on their own, though court support was valuable for revenue and 'royal' boxes in the 'royal' theatres were a common feature. In such cities the legitimate stage developed rather more freely. It was more to the popular taste, and while royal patronage was not unwelcome to writers it might be less essential.

The eighteenth century, starting from its earlier years, saw the evolution of star performers and their encouragement by princes. Audiences and princes went as much to see the actor as the spectacle, and the whole profession profited from this. Great singers and dancers were also courted, some even presented to the crown. Royals would attend their benefit performances, grant pensions and, more rarely, take the female leads as mistresses. For anyone, the claim to have performed before 'crowned heads' was billed as a guarantee of some significance and helped them in the provinces, even if the claim was not always strictly true.

At all times the princes could influence what was played. Thus French chauvinism bolstered up French plays whilst, diametrically opposed, Frederick the Great's distaste for German went some way to hold back the development of any native drama. He also hated Shakespeare whom he found intolerably vulgar, despising one who juxtaposed a gravedigger and a prince, although he himself as a general mixed among his soldiery with unconcern.

205

This Chelsea violinist could as well be the footman as a prince, *en déshabille,* practicing his part. Both might play together as amateurs. Royal composition was also quite a common phenomenon, as the score *(below)* of a concerto by the Princess Wilhelmine of Prussia, Margravine of Bayreuth, bears witness.

If we have stressed the theatre as apart from music, it is because, on the whole, the former was a fairly new development in absolutist courts. Kings and princes had always had musicians. They were a necessary part of the surroundings. Even the most philistine could appreciate a rousing march or hunting song and all had need of music for their fanfares, balls and dances. Besides, a handful of musicians was within the purse of any prince.

If there was any deeper development in baroque times it came together with the opera and ballet in an appreciation of more serious music. Chamber music had a ready following. Court musicians would perform on almost any evening that there was not gambling or some formal entertainment. In chamber music the amateurs found full expression. Royals, like other noble men and women, were allowed and usually encouraged to play if they had any interest. No instrument came amiss, as is illustrated in a picture of Graf Casimir zu Sayn-Wittgenstein-Berleburg which shows his princely family of seven each playing an instrument – flute, oboe, lute, harpsichord, horn, viola da gamba and violin. At such small centres the home performances were mostly all there was, and the common interest threw any members of the household into democratic amity to make quartets or chamber orchestras. The duke and the school-master, the duchess and the lackey thought no harm was done in sitting down together with the parson and the doctor or some local gentry, if they played. In larger courts the prince and princess joined their orchestras to play what part they pleased. Quite a number could compose as well.

All this activity helped music in general, not only soloists but composers too. We owe a great deal of our finest heritage to their efforts for special court occasions: the quartets and concerts and masses turned out for royal birthdays, marriages and deaths were legion. It is notable how quickly some of them were written. All this would have been impossible without princely help, as, apart from church organists, there was little gainful outlet for a man of talent unless in desultory teaching. Deprived of court support or attempting to freelance even an eminent composer could fare ill, as Mozart found.

These people also benefited socially, which counted much to them. The painters, writers or musicians to the court were almost 'gentlemen' and, when the new academies evolved, the most successful achieved riches, fame and some even orders and ennoblement. Dr Burney, as an organist, was able to arrange that his daughter could wait on the queen. She hated it and had a breakdown; he was quite transported with delight at such an honour.

Again, as with hunting, art received some stimulus from all this interest. Trophies and motifs of instruments and music continued among the most popular of decorative features of the time. They

Amateur theatricals were all the rage, as we see in this painting by Downman, which apparently shows the Prince of Wales, Charles James Fox and others at play.

are to be found in every material. The creation of fine instruments for court quartets and orchestras kept up a quite important patronage and helped the best in such professions. To be 'Maker' or 'Purveyor' to the king or Highness could assure the firms a handsome réclame for their business.

If, as indoor interests, the opera and theatre vied with gambling and balls for greatest favour, gambling would have won the vote with very many of the royals themselves. Almost everyone at court, men and women, gambled fantastically. They would lose in thousands not in hundreds, whatever the currency. They would pledge estates as readily as pocket money. Although it was not banned by any church, gambling was certainly not encouraged at

Right Significant of the importance of court patronage was the practice of dedicating compositions to a member of the court or highest aristocracy. The dedication in itself usually represented a gesture of thanks for some more practical support, rather than simply a grant of permission so to promote a work.

Opposite A game of lotto. Such a modest example, might seem a curious inclusion in a book about princes, but this particular set is significantly pertinent as it belonged to the little Dauphin at the time of the imprisonment of the French royal family before their execution in 1789.

LA MUSE LYRIQUE:
DÉDIÉE
A Madame
LA DAUPHINE.
IIII.ᵉ Recueil d'Airs
Avec Accompagnement de Guitarre,
PAR Mᴿ. PATOUART Fils.
Par Souscription.
A PARIS,
Chez JOLIVET *rue Françoise.*
AVEC PRIVILEGE DU ROY.

Prix de la Souscription
Pour Paris......................... 12ˡᵗ
Pour la Province, *franc de port*... 18

Although Gabriel Grupello may not have seen Johann Wilhelm von der Pfalz *(left)* as a beauty even of his period, nor indeed have carved his bust with the facility of a Bernini, he has recorded the features of a prince whose patronage was catholic and quite considerable. The musical relief in ivory *(above)* by Ignaz Elhafen and the elaborate viola da gamba *(right)* by Joachim Tielcke, 1691, belonged to the Prince, both the work of leading craftsmen in their fields.

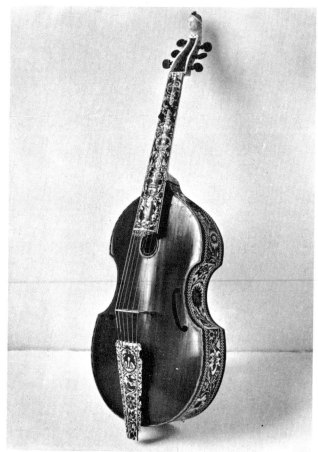

Sometimes the richest played for gold, at other times elaborate counters were used or, more simply, charming ivory sets as here.

the time, and gaming houses in the outside world were targets for denunciation in the strongest moral terms. Yet the courts went on and on. Far from playing it discreetly, they usually did so with the fullest royal participation and encouragement, at gaming tables set by royalty and with hospitality provided by the prince. This, at least, was the case in France and though some other princes were not so encouraging they seldom banned the practice.

From the Versailles standpoint, gambling was part and parcel of the whole design of leading nobles and courtiers to expend their time and money on such trivia instead of politics. It must be admitted that few required great encouragement, while for those with any instinct for the game, court practice made the vice respectable and countered any twinge of conscience that some earlier conditioning might have aroused. The dauphin's copybook counsels the avoidance of 'plaisirs funestes', of which eighteenth-century gambling might well be seen as one. Everywhere diaries and letters harp on this and on the casual nonchalance with which court gambling was so often carried on.

Many writers noticed the great gamblers like Dangeau and commented with surprise at his intensity of concentration and calculating determination to win, as though this were something out of the ordinary. But quite a number of the shadier members of the courts made a living from the tables and no doubt were helped by just this characteristic.

To be a 'good loser' might have been expected of a royal or nobleman, but, in fact, many of them were far from that and although some have gone down in history for their deadpan attitude and magnificent deportment on losing everything, many more would rant and rave and curse and swear with excitement as the game went on. Cheating, if not encouraged, was far from rare, even among princesses, for either sex indulged in this pastime as freely as they could.

Many princes and princesses were extremely glad to win, especially dependents, who were often short of cash or credit. Most just gambled because the opportunity was there and, then as now, even the richest loved it, though their winnings could mean nothing to their lives and often their losses came from national taxes anyway. Many are the records of appeals to parliament or finance ministers for funds to liquidate some princely debt to which so often gambling contributed.

Bets can, of course, be made on anything and always have been, but the fundamental games go right back into history and have altered only superficially. In England racing played its part, but on the continent the heavy gambling was on cards, with dice or primitive roulette-type games as secondary means. Chess or back-gammon gave an opportunity for those who liked to blend some gentle skill with luck. But nothing really matched the cards for royal favour. It is noteworthy that at certain courts the only time a man might sit before the king was when engaged on wagering his money with the sovereign.

Together with this encouraged dissipation, came formal entertainments at the courts, primarily balls and dances, for feasting, as such, was inhibited by the fact that ordinarily none could eat with Highnesses. Feasts were held at court only on special occasions, when they were likely to be for royals alone, and the company would stand for hours while princes and princesses toyed with courses by the dozen. Fanfares or even cannon announced the toast and all the etiquettes of court were brought to play. This cannot really have been looked upon as entertainment either for the royals concerned or for the court. Usually it was but a formal ritual entertaining of 'cousins' or the family.

A buffet hospitality usually accompanied gambling evenings, but for sitdown meals the best that ordinary visitors might get was feeding with the equerries or officials in attendance. This was general practice for reasonably well off touring foreigners, especially at small continental courts. But with or without further hospitality and entertainment, balls and dances were everywhere a feature of court life. Most princes liked them very much. It was a chance to dress up in their finest and surround themselves with all their highest subjects also tricked out in their best. In the greatest settings these spectacles of breeding, wealth and elegance, of jewellery and colour must indeed have been superlative.

If not the culminating point of the system, they were one of its most spectacular manifestations. Politically, they could be invaluable for the absolutist system. If the greatest subjects had to be attached by formal occupation to the court, invitations to the court affairs was enough to keep the generality in humble duty. As diaries recall, the women fought, intrigued, begged, bribed and went to any lengths for access to such parties.

Naturally every effort was made to give some twist of novelty and charm to any special party. Just as parks were replanted, lakes and boats pressed into service, so palace walls were newly decorated and transformed. Fancy dress was always popular, as court and courtiers played at gods and goddesses as well as shepherds and their shepherdesses. Some liked particularly to dress as peasants, and then the quality would come disguised as tinkers, tailors, farmers, beggars. Occasionally the Munich electors dressed as host and hostess publicans, speaking dialect, which all of course could use, and as barmen they entertained their peasant court. Once again the theatre entered into daily life and once again the cost was quite phenomenal, though possibly not so much for a fancy dress as for the formal court creations of official ceremony.

Hobbies

Apart from hunting, gambling and the theatre, some other interests and hobbies found their place in royal favour. Most significant for us, perhaps, was their collecting, which among baroque princes was as divergent and widespread as among the rich today.

Some were primarily interested in furniture or silver and objects for the palace, others also in a picture gallery or more recondite 'collectors' items'. From their home conditioning most princes had some feeling for the objects that made up their background, the cabinets and statues, furniture, and so on. At the outset the taste nearly always tended towards the heavy showy styles, and even when the period fashion changed to elegance and lightness in the later eighteenth century a number of the more old-fashioned still preferred the earlier styles.

As with other families, it was seldom that a passion for the arts or collecting descended regularly from one generation of royals to the next, but at the greatest courts collecting and patronage had become so much a part of royal life that they usually continued whether the actual sovereign was interested or not. Galleries and cabinets grew as successive librarians and curators gathered and hoarded up as best they might. Objects were acquired partly as a result of the generally accepted custom among cousins of sending items as exchanges or gifts, partly with the help of mistresses or queens, and by purchase. This last had to be delegated, even by the most serious royal collector. Agents, who might be dealers, or specially appointed emissaries, or often ambassadors with taste, had to make the purchases where opportunity occurred. It is remarkable how clearly the collections vary according to whether the buyer had real taste or not. A particularly felicitous ambassadorial arrangement was made for Sweden by the younger Tessin. The resulting group of French paintings, and above all drawings, reflects the most penetrating judgment in its field. There was no question of taking an aeroplane to view a sale, a possibility which makes – or can make – twentieth-century collecting so much more personal. Where royal collections are personal it is likely to have been due to the individual taste of a librarian or an agent trusted by the prince. Occasionally, as with Frederick the Great, an intensely intimate selection appears, but in general, these cabinets

The curiosities of far off lands might often be mounted for princely collectors into objects of contemporary appeal. This splendid gold and enamel *JuJu* was created by Dinglinger around an ancient Mexican jade mask, which is the only original part. On the one hand the extravagance of the setting betokens the value and interest in the jade; at the same time the cheerful lack of respect for untouched originality, which has become such a fetish with 20th-century collectors, is almost shocking. The delicious fantasy of this fearsome deity is in full accord with the taste for chinoiserie and bears witness to yet another aspect of 18th-century attitudes.

give the impression of having been amassed under little more than general guidance. Dutch pictures of the previous hundred years and Italian baroque were very popular in Germany, Gothic virtually not at all. Certain outstanding artists like Poussin, Raphael, Titian, stood out as royal 'musts' for galleries of any real pretension.

Occasionally, collections were bought up en bloc and even made by dealers for the purpose. George III's purchase of Venetian paintings and drawings from Consul Smith presents a case in point, as indeed does Catherine the Great's buying of all Walpole's pictures. The National Gallery in London owes its foundation to the acquisition of a block of pictures got together for a royal, who died before the gallery could be exported.

The comparative rarity of good pictures outside the major royal collections is often attributed to expense, but this does not really seem to be true. Certainly some contemporaries were well paid, but by and large, apart from very fashionable paintings a fine collection could have been made for less than the cost of a few evenings' opera or parties.

The two manuscripts *(opposite)* afford a pleasantly intimate view of serious royal collecting. At the top is a page from a catalogue of purchases by Nicodemus Tessin on behalf of the Swedish crown. The list is catholic and a visit today to the galleries in Stockholm bears eloquent testimony to the taste with which this artistic ambassador made his selections. Below, opposite charming studies in his sketchbook, Sir Joshua Reynolds noted down art objects that he saw in Florence, the great majority, of course, due to Medici patronage. Another facet of royal collecting, and one perhaps more common in the smaller courts, was the practice of having prints or miniature copies of great works set in highly elaborate frames or patterns to make decoration for a room. In the Miniature Room in the Munich Residenz *(right)* we have a supreme example of the taste and care spent by Cuvilliés and Dietrich around 1730 on beautiful framing for dozens of very indifferent little pictures.

Certainly the absence of fine paintings (apart from ceilings) in so costly and so exquisite a house as Brühl is notable, as is often the elaboration of the frames for quite indifferent works. The comparative indifference to artistic merit in historical assemblages at other centres seems to reveal the same attitude.

The quality of 'curiosity', rather than artistic beauty, dominated many tastes and is manifest in the appreciation of the detail in Dutch paintings. The cruder comments in the genre scenes, or the drops of water on the leaves, or flies on fruit made points for comment on the obvious and demanded nothing of the intellect.

217

Landscapes and battle scenes were openly evocative. Later, with the advance of education and the evolution of the cult for 'finer feelings', gushing or even tearful outlet could be found before some harrowing presentation. Often what seem to us just pretty figures in nice costumes had a true emotional significance.

Sculpture – mainly classical – could always find a place, though seldom on the patterned scale of Munich's Residenz. Contemporory sculptures were rather an adjunct to the architecture or the general setting than collected for their own intrinsic contribution. Busts, like portraits, were more often looked at for their subject than their art. Good, or where the purse or influence afforded, the best contemporary sculptors were commissioned to make busts and monuments, and most princes liked to keep a sculptor and a painter at their court. Occasionally they went outside, like Charles I, who sent a three-way portrait to Bernini so that the sculptor might do a bust from it. Louis XIV, with greater wealth, summoned Bernini to France, where he treated him with great magnificence, and commissioned him to execute a monument and to design a palace.

For royals who liked the more patterned type of collecting with series for completion, books, prints, coins, medals or cameos, served roughly in that order. These presented outlets that had remained in favour through the centuries. Ceramics, too, had been collected, and a special vogue for them had developed, as more and more was imported from the east. This passion was given even wider scope in the eighteenth century, when many princes had their own supported manufactories. Objects with classical association like tomb inscriptions, vases, funerary urns and so on also had a fascination for the time.

In every palace 'curiosities' had great popularity and their appeal was general. Ranging from highly speculative semi-magical things like 'unicorn horns' (narwhal to us), through meteorites or fossils, shells and minerals, given curious attributions, the different items could always make some point for wonder or for conversation even if aesthetics did not come into the discussion. Appreciation was then more general and simple. By the same token, travellers' souvenirs were attractive. To a very circumscribed world these touchstones of the outside globe, or spheres beyond, had something of the quality of the religious relics that were still so eagerly sought after. Such pieces could be given fabulous associations and tales which no one could deny. Arms and armour, like relics of the chase, had a readily appreciable attraction and usually showed some family or personal association which made them even more desirable.

Whatever field of interest became involved, the possession of a 'cabinet of art and wonder' had become essential as a prestige

This charming life-size group by Antonio Corradini was commissioned by Augustus the Strong about 1725. It stands here as representative of the whole area of patronage which could be exercized by princes of taste. Without their support the world's artistic heritage would have been a vast deal poorer.

Opposite, The Elector Max Emanuel relaxes. The portrait *(centre)* shows him still attended by a standing nobleman although about to start ivory turning on his lathe. Above is the actual tool, made by Coustou in 1712 in Paris, where the Elector was in exile at the time. It bears his coat-of-arms of course. Below, the ivory chandelier is said to have been turned by a princely amateur, possibly even this Elector.

Below This exquisite ivory cabinet was made in the early 17th century by Christof Angermeier to hold the princely coin collection of the Wittelsbachs.

adjunct for an eighteenth-century prince. Even if individual appreciation might be quixotic, such assemblages were a source of pride, and visitors to them encouraged as an excuse to show them off. At smaller courts the prince himself might sometimes do the honours if there was likelihood of scholarly exchange. The visits were ordinarily leisurely and gave occasion for displays of knowledge and at least they passed more time. In quite a number, the curators sought a tip for opening up and guiding wealthy tourists.

In addition to what might be termed inside collections, the seventeenth and particularly the eighteenth century, saw wide development of zoos and menageries. The former were normally restricted to the more portable fauna, such as ducks and geese from far away. These collections were always a point for visitors and a goal to which parties of residents could stroll. Botanical gardens, though less widespread, were founded and encouraged by many kings and princes.

Other hobbies of royals were as varied as those of any commoner but perhaps amateur science and amateur mechanics, together with crafts like clockmaking and ivory-turning, had pride of place. The science might range from outright alchemy and near

astrology to serious astronomy, or else be restricted to messing about with alembics as a child might play at 'stinks'. When the Highnesses were serious, often very beautiful apparatus was made for them to play with and the cabinets of tools or lathes or scientific instruments supplied by leading jewellers. Many princes like Frederick the Great were very proud of their laboratories and often sought to collect fine old instruments like astrolabes.

In all these fields it was probable that for the majority of princes the chief interest lay in what may be termed the personal or historical or literary, rather than the aesthetic, aspects of the things they had. Portraits or even personal items were prized for their family associations, while objects like rhinoceros horns afforded a mixture of magic, far off lands and strange wonder. An indication of this approach is given by 'cabinets' that have remained more or less intact, like that in Rosenberg Castle. Here works of art, which may be of considerable charm and value, stand cheek by jowl on shelves with native beads or knick-knacks, little family presents, nursery offerings or wedding souvenirs.

Almost everyone was fascinated by technical dexterity and as the eighteenth century progressed it became almost of first consequence in works of art. The more elaborately turned the ivory cup the better, especially if it was executed by a princely amateur. The more 'trompe l'œil' the scagliola table or finicky the inlay on a cabinet the more they were enjoyed. For the majority of royal collectors the most elaborate represented the best that wealth and consequence could buy and such pieces took their place alongside jewels as a fitting adjunct to royal life. Étuis, snuff boxes, watches were eagerly sought and many princes had the finest by the dozen. Especially elaborate casework and contrivances in clocks attracted royal patronage for gifts or purchase. Whether at a large capital, or modest court, the finest local makers and purveyors would generally attract royal patronage with all its consequent advantages for trade and social position.

In addition to these personal concerns came the wider interests in all such fields, and, apart from opera and theatre, the period saw a marked development in what we now regard as public patronage. For example, the mid-seventeenth century saw the foundation of a number of national 'schools' for painters and sculptors, especially at Rome. By the eighteenth century a growth of intellectual societies and academies sprang up under direct royal patronage. At these the more intelligent royals would attend personally and some even participate in the sessions or read papers.

It is significant for example that a small work like the *Storia del Anno 1765*, though published some twenty years later when these things had become even more *de rigueur*, should devote several lines of its obituary of Francis of Lorraine, consort of Maria

Unhappily a taste for finicky elaboration of detail had more appeal for many royals than beauty. This detail in the marquetry of the bureau made by Riesener for King Stanislas of Poland in 1760 is a case in point.

Theresa, to the fact that he had 'encouraged research for the public advantage, introduced manufactures and improved those already established, constructed a number of Institutions for the advantage of the State, including a Museum of Natural History, which even today [1783] remains a matter for stupefaction'. The current passion for numismatics is also recorded in congratulating Francis on his collection of 'all moneys coined since Charlemagne, which affords a consecutive metallic record of history and provides a monument as serviceable to chronology as it is worthy of a Great Sovereign. He also created marvellous gardens where may be seen the plants, trees and fruits of the New World.' The entry then concludes that 'he lacked for nothing in War or Peace', and that Austria had been 'fortunate in having a Prince of such an equable, beneficent, magnanimous and compassionate nature'. Such things as these were what enlightened monarchs sought to do.

In the same vein but perhaps more pertinently significant for us today was the action of Anna Maria Ludovica, the last direct heir of the Medici, whose Tuscan heritage had been taken over by the emperor. Determined that as little as possible should go to the grasping Austrians, she bequeathed the whole vast art collections of the Medici to the city of Florence with the immensely intelligent rider that they should never be alienated and should be held there not only for the Tuscans but 'for all foreigners from all over the world'. The size and scope of this bequest is truly staggering, when we consider that it included, among other things, the galleries of the Pitti and Uffizi.

Elsewhere other public collections were being brought together, though not always from a direct princely heritage. The British Museum, opened in 1760, had its 'royal' collections, but some of these inherited from George III were in fact a payment for the debts incurred by George, his regent son.

At a time of such general interests and advances in learning it is not surprising that the more intelligent monarch princes like Frederick the Great or Catherine sought personal contacts and even friendship with encyclopaedists such as d'Alembert or Diderot, or writers and thinkers from Voltaire to the blue-stocking Mme Geoffrin, even though she could not be received at Versailles, not being of noble birth. This condescension benefited many lesser dilettante travellers as we have seen in the case of Boswell, who could find a welcome at most princely centres through which he passed, by virtue of some contribution to the wider intellectual life. These were some of the good things of an autocratic power and independence. Certainly the best of baroque rulers would have been content to be remembered in the terms used by a diarist to describe an elector palatine: He was Magnificent, Generous, Liberal, a Protector of the Arts.

Postscript

This book does not pretend to be a study in detail of any individual, and only on the broadest lines does it attempt to review a period. We have tried rather to convey something of the attitudes of European princes and their entourages in the seventeenth and eighteenth centuries, whose influence has permeated right down to our own times.

Certainly at the opening of this century, and even today, in conformity or opposition, most of the world has been deeply affected by their heritage. The concern is not only with monarchy itself, but with many basic attitudes to social life. With the spread of affluence more and more of the affectations of rococo privilege have been adapted – or perverted – by other classes. Our structure of snobberies on either side of the Atlantic and in areas that feel our influence is in essence that of the princes, except that money can now take the place of birth. By 1919 the last of the robust, age-old heritage of folk tradition in dress, behaviour or even fun had been discarded almost everywhere. Only in the last decade has youth sought again a general independent pattern of its own. Between the wars, apart from small minorities, it was pastiche pompadours – mostly of flawless virtue – who trod the ballrooms from industrial suburbs to the tropic shanty towns, in imitation of the eighteenth century as they imagined it, while their elders might take tea in straight-backed, stiff formality derived from salons of two centuries before. All this was not a middle-class prerogative. For many, natural speech or manners were sacrificed in favour of some affectation of superiority. Even today few of the most truculent supporters of egalitarian democracy remain content to be the 'men' or 'woman' that they are, but must needs be 'Gentlemen' and 'Ladies', whether on the public platform or the public lavatory. Whether this be for good or ill, an advance or decadence, it does not change the fact that we draw heavily upon the practices these leaders of our ancestors evolved. How this all came about is what we hope to have shown.

Acknowledgements

The photograph on page 70/2 is reproduced by gracious permission of H. M. the Queen. The author and publishers wish to thank the following museums and collections for permission to reproduce objects in their possession:

The Marquess of Cholmondeley, *page 63/1*; The Duke of Devonshire, 59; Lord Lonsdale, 71; Lord Radnor, 155; M. Lucien Baszanger, 112/*1*; Peter Coats Esq., 124-5; Mr and Mrs Charles Wrightsman, 112/*2*; Messrs P. and D. Colnaghi, 156; Heim Gallery (London) Ltd, 132/*2*; Private Collections, 25, 60, 62, 63/*2*, 82, 132/*1*, 178/*1*, 180, 207.

ALTÖTTING, Wallfahrtskapelle, 89/*2*, 92; AMSTERDAM, Rijksmuseum, 86; AUGUSTUSBURG, Schloss, 174; BESANÇON, Musée des Beaux-Arts, 128; BIRMINGHAM, City Art Gallery, 195/*1*; CAMBRIDGE, Fitzwilliam Museum, 203; COLOGNE, Wallraf-Richartz Museum, 133/*1*; COPENHAGEN, Slot Rosenborg, 17, 78, 102/*1*, 103/*1*; DRESDEN, Grünes Gewölbe, 56, 103/*2*, 104, 123, 126, 187/*3*; Historisches Museum, 135, 189; FLORENCE, Cappelle Medicee, 168/*2*; Galleria degli Arazzi, 11; Galleria degli Uffizi, 32, 33; Palazzo Riccardi, 44/*3*; FULDA, Schloss Fasanerie, 196, 197; GREENWICH, Royal Hospital, 4; KREMSMÜNSTER, Abbey (by courtesy of His Grace the Abbot), 167; LONDON, British Museum, 216/*2*; Kensington Palace (Crown copyright), 141; National Portrait Gallery, 37, 118 (B. M. loan); National Trust (Ickworth House), 121; Science Museum, 84/*1*; Victoria and Albert Museum (Crown copyright), 30/*1*, 36, 39/*1*, 39/*2*, 44/*1*, 54/*1*, 54/*2*, 64, 70/*1*, 131, 140/*2*, 144, 150/*1*, 150/*2*, 151, 157, 158, 175/*3*, 187/*1*, 194/*1*, 194/*2*, 194/*3*, 199, 202, 206/*1*, 218; Wallace Collection (Crown copyright), 108, 111, 161, 185, 190, 222; Westminster Abbey (by courtesy of the Dean and Chapter), 21, 96/*2*; MADRID, Prado, 66; MUNICH, Bayerisches Nationalmuseum, 12, 23/*1*, 30/*2*, 46/*1*, 81/*2*, 133/*3*, 175/*2*, 178/*2*, 210, 211/*1*, 211/*2*, 212, 220; Bayerische Staatsgemäldesammlungen, 89/*1*; Deutsches Jagdmuseum, 193; Residenz, 46/*2*, 47, 142, 217; (Schatzkammer), 3, 8, 61, 102/*3*, 166, 214; Schloss Nymphenburg, 221/*1*, 221/*2*, 221/*3*; (Marstallmuseum), 146; NAPLES, Palace of Capodimonte, 97; NUREMBERG, Germanisches Museum, 38, 50; OXFORD, Ashmolean Museum, 186; PARIS, Archives de France, 136; Bibliothèque Nationale, 113, 168/*1*; Bibliothèque Ste-Geneviève, 209; Musée des Arts Décoratifs, 69, 80, 107, 133/*2*; Musée Carnavalet, 81/*3*, 208; Musée du Louvre, 18, 110, 139/*1*, 140/*1*; Musée Nissim de Camondo, 138; PAVLOVSK, Palace, 182; ROME, Quirinal Palace, 96/*1*; ROTTAM-INN, Former Abbey Church, 94, 164; SÈVRES, Musée National de Céramique, 139/*2*; STOCKHOLM, Royal Library, 216/*1*; Swedish Treasury, 91; TURIN, Church of La Consolata, 117; Museo Civico, 192; Royal Palace, 49/*2*; VENICE, Palazzo Mocenigo Stae, 100; VERSAILLES, Musée National, 99; Musée Lambinet, 102/*2*, 103/*3*; VIENNA, Heeresgeschichtliches Museum, 187/*2*; Historisches Museum der Stadt, *endpapers*; Kunsthistorisches Museum, 10, 81/*1*, 84/*2*, 85, 88, 115; (Schloss Schönbrunn), 52, 149, 200; (Wagenburg), 148; Nationalbibliothek, 163; WALDSASSEN, Abbey 171; WOLFENBÜTTEL, Herzog-August Bibliothek, 206/*2*.

Photographs were kindly supplied by the abovementioned museums and collections and by the following (colour plates are shown in **bold type**): Alinari, 11, 32, 33, 44/*2*, 44/*3*, 49/*2*, 96/*1*, 97, 117, 168/*2*; Archives Photographiques, 99; Bayerische Verwaltung der staatlichen Schlösser, Gärten und Seen, **3**, **8**, 46/*2*, **47**, **61**, 142, 146, 166, 175/*1*, 179/*1*, 195/*2*, 205/*2*, 214, 217, 221/*1*, 221/*2*, 221/*3*; Bildarchiv der österreichischen Nationalbibliothek, 163, 169; Trustees of the Chatsworth Settlement, 59; Lucca Chmel, 45/*1*, 48; Josip Ciganovic-Omnikus, 24/*2*; Commune di Venezia (Direzione di Belle Arti), 100; A. C. Cooper, 86, 89/*2*, 180; John Dayton, **101**; Deutscher Kunstverlag (Walter Hege), 43; (Fritz Thudichum), 22; Kerry Dundas, **73**; Electa Editore, **113**; Françoise Foliot, 81/*3*, 102/*2*, 103/*3*, **136**, **208**; Werner Forman, 51, 168/*3*; J. R. Freeman, 150/*1*, 150/*2*, 151, 156, 157; Giraudon, 168/*1*, 184, 209; Photo-Verlag Gundermann, 177; Claus Hansmann, **17**, **26**, **56**, **91**, **92**, **102/*1***, 102/*3*, **103/*1***, 103/*2*, **104**, **123**, **126**, **135**, **187/*3***, **189**; André Held, 66, **153**; Josse-Lalance, **18**; F. L. Kennet, 21, 164; Foto Marburg, 20; Erwin Meyer, 187/*2*; National Trust (O. G. Jarman), 121; Nakladatelství Orbis, 205/*1*; Réalités (M. Nahmias), 138, 139/*2*; Hans Retzlaff, 196, 197; Royal Academy of Arts, 63, 112/*2*, 133/*1*; Schmölz-Huth, 45/*2*; Toni Schneiders (Buch-Kunstverlag Ettal), 24/*1*; Edwin Smith, 40, 49/*1*, **55**, **74**, **114**, **154**, **172**; Städtische Kunstsammlungen, Augsburg, 167; Státní ústav památkové péče a ochrany přírody (Soňa Divišová), 23/*2*; (Vladimir Hyhlík), 198; Dr Johannes Steiner, **171**; Harold C. Tilzey, 162; Victoria and Albert Museum photo (Crown copyright), 50, 71, 94, 96/*2*, 174, 178/*2*, 179/*2*, Derrick Witty, **4**.